2020

Dear Melis,

We both know God is always working all 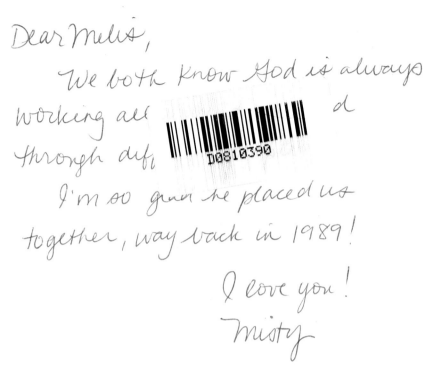 d through diff

I'm so gran he placed us together, way back in 1989!

I love you!

Misty

More Than Coincidence

More Than Coincidence

When God Shines His Light on You

EDITORS OF GUIDEPOSTS

MJF BOOKS
NEW YORK

Published by MJF Books
Fine Communications
322 Eighth Avenue
New York, NY 10001

More Than Coincidence
LC Control Number: 2015946502
ISBN 978-1-60671-324-2

This book was previously published as *Heaven Sent*.

Acknowledgments:

Every attempt has been made to credit the sources of copyrighted material used in this book.
If any such acknowledgment has been inadvertently omitted or miscredited, receipt of such
information would be appreciated.

Scripture quotations marked (KJV) are taken from the King James Version of the Bible.

Scripture quotations marked (NAS) are taken from the *New American Standard Bible*, copyright
© 1960, 1962, 1963, 1968, 1971, 1972, 1973, 1975, 1977, 1995 by the Lockman Foundation.
Used by permission.

Scripture quotations marked (NIV) are taken from *The Holy Bible, New International Version*.
Copyright © 1973, 1978, 1984, 2011 by Biblica, Inc. Used by permission of Zondervan. All
rights reserved worldwide. www.zondervan.com

Scripture quotations marked (NKJV) are taken from *The Holy Bible, New King James Version*.
Copyright © 1982 by Thomas Nelson, Inc.

Scripture quotations marked (RSV) are taken from the *Revised Standard Version of the Bible*.
Copyright © 1946, 1952, 1971 by Division of Christian Education of the National Council of
Churches of Christ in the United States of America. Used by permission.

Scripture quotations marked (TLB) are taken from *The Living Bible*. Copyright © 1971 by
Tyndale House Publishers, Wheaton, IL 60187. All rights reserved.

This edition is published by MJF Books in arrangement with Guideposts.

QF   10 9 8 7 6 5 4 3 2 1

CONTENTS

CHAPTER 4: YOU WILL BE HEALED

CHAPTER 5: THE LORD DIRECTS YOUR STEPS

CHAPTER 6: ALL THINGS BECOME NEW

CHAPTER 7: IN THE HANDS OF GOD

CHAPTER 8: REVEALED IN VISIONS

INTRODUCTION

"Never will I leave you; never will I forsake you" (Hebrews 13:5, NIV). Time and again we see evidence that reveals God's involvement in our everyday lives. Sometimes the heaven-sent guidance is overlooked when we brush it off as coincidence. Other times, we can think of it as nothing less than a miracle.

Van Varner, the former editor of *Guideposts* magazine, wrote, "Faith is made of mystery and awe; it is not in knowing the tangible but in believing in the intangible that our faith flourishes. The hidden hand of God moves silently, leaving behind the evidence of things unseen."

This is the very idea this book explores: it is in those moments, when we see God's mysterious touch in our lives, that our faith is the strongest. Though we can't always understand His methods, we know that He is directing us toward the right path or helping us through the tough times.

More Than Coincidence compiles stories from the best-loved column in *Guideposts* magazine, Mysterious Ways, and from *Mysterious Ways* magazine to reveal the surprising spiritual strength that emerges when people find that God is right there with them in every type of situation: from a chocolate cake that arrived at just the right moment to two sisters made invisible in a time of great danger. You will see yourself—and find positive new perspective on your situation—in eighty stories from people who have encountered the mysterious and divine in their own lives.

Rita Turner takes you through the surprising circumstances that led her, at the age of sixty-two, to leave behind her comfortable and familiar surroundings and travel to China to teach English as part of a master's degree program. Eileen Helm Fulton reveals how a chance encounter on vacation blooms into friendship and allows her to help save a man's life. Jack Brewer realizes God has a continuing purpose for him when a boy visits him in a dream and asks the question, "But what about me?"

Many other contributors acknowledge the surprising kindling of spiritual strength that happens when God influences their lives through heaven-sent comfort, protection, healing, and rejuvenation. Their gracious, thoughtful insights remind us that even in life's toughest moments, God has a plan for us.

While you read these stories, we hope that your faith is strengthened as you remember that God is at work in our lives and circumstances. We can trust Him for everything.

—Editors of Guideposts

More Than
Coincidence

CHAPTER 1

Inspiration from Above

LOST AND FOUND IN PARIS
by *Aminda Parafinik*

My heart pounded. My hands were clammy. I was on the verge of panic. The tangle of multicolored lines on the Paris Métro map made my head spin. I asked a ticket-booth attendant for help. He shot me a dismissive look. How could I have been so careless? The world never felt so big, and I never felt so small, so lost. I'd come to Paris in hopes of finding myself. Now I couldn't even find my way back to my hostel.

"If you're lost in Paris, just look for the Eiffel Tower," another traveler told me when I arrived from Arizona. If only there were a guidepost to help me find my way in life! Two months earlier, I'd been downsized from my job as an editorial assistant, my second job since graduating from college with a degree in communications. I'd thought I would be climbing the ranks by twenty-five. Instead, I was out of work. I felt like a loser.

I dreamed of getting away. That's when I got the idea for this trip. I'd been fascinated by "the City of Light" ever since I was a little girl. I had some money saved up. What better place was there to be inspired again?

I took in the awesome views from the top of the Eiffel Tower, gawked at the luxury shops along the Champs-Élysées, saw the magnificent Palace of Versailles. Today, though, after exploring exhibits at the Louvre and visiting the gargoyles at Notre Dame, I'd taken a wrong turn. The narrow streets surrounding the cathedral were like a maze. In the spirit of adventure, I kept going…until it got dark. I could see the Eiffel Tower, a finger of light impossibly distant. I searched for more than an hour until I found what I thought was the right Métro stop, but it was for a different line than the one that let off near my hostel.

I turned away from the ticket booth and the reality of my situation hit me. I'd been crazy to spend my savings on this trip, trying to "find myself." When—or if—I got home, then what? "Lord," I whispered, "please help me. I am so lost."

"*Excusez moi.*" A tall, brown-haired man startled me. A little older than me, clean-cut, dressed like a businessman. "Can I help you?" he asked, with just a hint of a French accent.

"I need to get to Félix Faure," I said, trying to keep my voice from quivering.

"Follow me," he said. Normally I wouldn't, but there was something about him. He seemed trustworthy. Confident. Besides, did I have a choice?

Striding through the dark streets, we made small talk. "Where are you from?" he asked. "The United States, obviously," he added, smiling. "But where?"

"Phoenix," I said. "It's in Arizona, the Southwest..."

"Really?" he interrupted. "Have you heard of the Thunderbird School of Global Management?"

I vaguely remembered that name from a billboard near my freeway exit. Of all the things in Phoenix to ask about. "I don't really know much about it," I said.

He paused, then looked at me quizzically as if he wanted to continue. But by then we'd reached the Métro line I needed. "Hurry, you don't want to miss your train," he said. I thanked him, then dashed down the stairs. Before long, I was back at the hostel. The rest of my time in Paris was uneventful, even restful. Something about that encounter seemed to calm me.

Okay, time to get back to my life. My first week home, I sent out more résumés. Nothing.

That weekend, I was scanning the want ads when a position caught my eye. They needed someone with a communications degree, and the responsibilities matched what I'd done in the past. Program assistant for an executive MBA program. I liked the sound of that.

I liked the sound of the employer too. The Thunderbird School of Global Management. Suddenly, the world seemed very small. I applied and was called in for an interview.

Guess who got the job?

GRANDPA AND THE GIANT TOMATO
by Denise Valuk

Everything's bigger in Texas, right? But the giant Beefmaster tomato that appeared in my garden one summer day was like nothing I'd ever seen. It was a real beauty—red, without a blemish. It bent the vine to the ground. How had I missed it earlier? I checked my garden at least twice a day. This behemoth had seemingly appeared overnight.

I plucked my prize and brought it inside to weigh it. Two pounds! My mouth watered. I thought of making salsa or jam, or simply slicing it, with salt...

Suddenly, a thought took hold of me and wouldn't let go. *Give the tomato to Grandpa.*

What? That seemed like a bad idea. Grandpa lived on a farm just a few miles away, but I hadn't seen him since Grandma's funeral. And for good reason. At the service more than one person commented, "That woman was a saint for putting up with him all those years." The dirt had barely settled on the coffin when he groused, "When are we eating? Ma's buried, let's get on with it." He was offensive and insensitive. You never knew what would come out of his mouth, but you knew you wouldn't like it.

I'd figured that out when I was a kid. The farm was paradise—one hundred acres of cornfields, cattle and, best of all, a huge vegetable garden. Grandma always greeted me at the door. "C'mon over here and let's make some cookies," she'd say, gently taking my hand and leading me to the kitchen. We baked, hung laundry, and cooked. Grandpa? He stayed out back, working the land. I knew, even then, that farming was incredibly demanding, and watching him fostered my own love of gardening.

Still, I longed for a hello, a wink, a "thanks for coming." Something. Then one day, I got it.

"How much was that?" he said with a scowl, pointing to my new car. "What do you need a brand-new vehicle for? Plenty of used ones out there!"

"Just ignore him, he doesn't mean any harm," Grandma said.

But his remarks hurt. Didn't he even want to know me? I was his granddaughter, for crying out loud!

I only visited in order to stay close to Grandma. Now that she was gone there was no reason to go out there. It certainly didn't matter to Grandpa. So why was I standing in my kitchen with an incredible urge to give him this amazing tomato? It didn't make sense.

And yet I couldn't bring myself to slice into it. I tried but I just couldn't do it. I was so frustrated that I finally surrendered. I took the tomato, got in my car, and drove to Grandpa's farm.

When I arrived, Grandpa was on his four-wheeler, riding in from the fields. Under his hat his face was a weathered mask carved by the elements and by years of working in the Texas heat, but at eighty-four, he was showing no signs of slowing down.

Must be that nasty temper of his that keeps him going, I thought. I got out of my car and stood there in the scorching summer sun, waiting for him to acknowledge my presence.

"What are you doing here?" he finally asked, cutting the engine. So much for a hello.

"Hi, Grandpa," I said, trying to sound cheerful, or at least civil. "I just stopped by to see how you've been doing."

"Well," he said, stepping down from the four-wheeler, "now that Ma's gone, I have to do all the cooking and cleaning. And I think someone has been stealing corn from the field...."

I wiped the sweat off my forehead and tried to tune out his complaining. I opened the passenger door and hauled out the tomato.

"Hey, Grandpa! Look at this guy!" I bragged, holding up my prized fruit.

He gave it a cursory glance and stared out into the fields. "So? I've got a whole garden full of those."

"Of course," I said, lowering the tomato to my side. "You grow great tomatoes."

"I need to get to the cows. No time to visit," he said.

He climbed back on the four-wheeler and sped off so quickly that gravel flew in every direction. I contemplated flinging my precious tomato after him.

Now it didn't seem so impressive. More like a symbol of futility. I couldn't wait to get rid of it. I ducked into Grandpa's house, dropped the tomato on the counter and bolted. Maybe the old guy would eat it. Maybe not. I didn't care. The next time I had a strange urge, I planned to ignore it.

A few days later, Grandpa's number showed up on my caller ID. He'd never called me before. Never. I braced myself, thinking it would be horrible news from a friend or relative phoning from his house.

"Hello...," I said.

"How did you get that tomato so dang big? You use Miracle-Gro or somethin'?"

"Huh? Grandpa?"

"That giant tomato you brought? How the dickens did you get it so big?" he asked. "I ain't never grown one nowhere near that big and I've been growing tomatoes for seventy years!" His voice was gruff, but for the first time I detected a hint of friendliness, like he was trying. And maybe a little lonely without Grandma. I knew how that felt.

"Well, I always put a lot of manure in my garden," I explained, maybe a little smugly. "I don't like to use any chemicals."

"I ate on that tomato for days. And it was good. Real good."

Was that a compliment?

"Next time," he said, "call first, so we can go in the house and talk for a while, spend some time."

I almost dropped the phone. "Okay, I will," I promised.

And I did. I called Grandpa regularly after that and visited him often. He was still a tough old Texas farmer, but on the inside, his heart seemed to have grown overnight. Just like the largest tomato I'd ever seen.

WORDS THAT WEREN'T THERE
by Jim Hinch

The creeks were bone dry. For two days I hiked past one dusty stream-
bed after another, deeper into the backcountry of Yosemite National Park.
Here near the headwaters of the Merced River, miles away and thousands
of feet above where the rapids plunge into fabled Yosemite Valley, there
should have been plenty of water to refill my bottle. Instead, nothing.

My wife, Kate, usually backpacked these trails with me, but she understood I needed some time to myself, to sort out my jumbled feelings. The
wilderness is where I've always felt spiritually at peace, closer to understanding the hills and valleys of my own life. I wanted to hear God say He
cared. About me. About my mother.

After several years of winning her longtime battle against alcoholism,
my mom had relapsed. Badly. She'd called me, telling me she'd driven her
car off the freeway. That she only got a DUI and didn't kill someone was
nothing short of a miracle. How could my mom, in her seventies and
grandmother to my two kids, be sitting in jail, drunk? Now she was shakily
attending Alcoholics Anonymous meetings again. I blamed God for not
shielding my mom and everyone else in our family from the terrible toll
of addiction. Her latest setback opened old wounds. Painful memories of
fear and shame I'd long tried to bury. If God was truly just, how could He
allow this?

I swished the last drops of water around in my bottle, feeling more
desolate, more forsaken, than before I'd left. A friend and I hiking this
same trail had once traversed snowfields and waded through roaring creeks
with our boots off. Not today. A record drought had struck California.
The creek where I'd planned to make camp was nothing but dusty earth. I
finished off my water and gazed into the blank blue sky.

Keep going or turn back? I'd camped the night before beside the trick-ling outflow from a lake. But that was miles in the other direction, and it would be dark soon. No, I had to forge ahead, and hope the creek held water higher up.

I trudged on, increasingly uneasy as shadows lengthened and the creek bed stayed dry. At last I came to where a tributary joined the creek from a cleft in the granite mountainside, but instead of a roiling meeting of the waters all I found were some stagnant pools. I could hike for another hour before it got dark, but… *This is the best it will get,* I thought. *Why go on?*

I hastily put up my tent, pumped some murky water through a porta-ble filter, and cooked dinner. But I wasn't hungry. There was a knot in my stomach, and it wasn't from dehydration. I closed my eyes and pictured my mom in one of her AA meetings, invoking a higher power to help her overcome her own desperate thirst, conquer the urge that led her again and again to hurt herself and others. Was anyone listening?

Wiping off the dust, I crawled into my tent and zipped my sleeping bag. I tried saying evening prayers with the prayer book I'd brought, but the words died on my cracked lips. I took out the other book in my backpack, C. S. Lewis's *Mere Christianity,* a reliable favorite, and opened to a random page. *The plain fact is, God is good. He hates evil and injustice and He does everything He can to put them right. He is not some indifferent moral force. He cares very much what individual people do, right here and right now.*

I stared at the page. I'd read this book many times, but I didn't remember that passage. Not at all. Probably because I hadn't needed those particular words before now. I read the passage over and over, letting the message sink in: *He cares very much.*

At last I marked the page, laid the book on my chest and gazed out-side. The ravine was pitch-black, and stars shimmered above. A small, fragile bubble of protection seemed to emanate from the book on my chest and surround me. All else was dark—the night, the dry creek, my mom's addiction, memories of growing up in an alcoholic home. I wanted those words in the book to be true. To know for sure that the power my mother was looking to for her recovery was real.

I awoke before sunrise, ate breakfast, and packed up. I couldn't get away from that dry creek fast enough. There were ten miles and a ten thousand-foot pass to traverse before I reached my car. I filtered two bottles full of the stagnant water and hurried along the trail, beginning a steep, rocky ascent. Before long the trail leveled out. My eye caught a flash of color in the distance. A vibrant green. What was this? A mirage?

Ahead, the trail cut a path through a lush meadow. Aspen leaves spun. Swishing through the tall grass I smelled rich earth and the pungent scent of wildflowers. I heard a trickling sound—water! Somehow, drought hadn't touched this place! If I'd just hiked a few more miles the night before, I'd have had all that I needed to fill my bottle.

A powerful force almost knocked me over. The flow of the creek, the smell of the mud and the flowers—everything grew crushingly intense. *Could sobriety be further along my mom's trail too?* The thought came so suddenly. *Will she find exactly what she needs if she keeps pushing on?* Finally, I allowed myself to hope. I began to cry. I couldn't help it. The entire meadow seemed to ring out the words I'd read the night before.

"You are good," I said out loud. "You do care. You do hate evil and injustice and You do try to put them right."

When I reached the parking lot I whipped out my cell phone to call Kate. Mountain climbers arranging their gear stared in bemusement as I breathlessly recounted my hike.

"Let me read you those words from *Mere Christianity*," I said, fumbling to pry the book from my backpack. I flipped to the page I'd marked the night before.

"That's weird," I said. "I know I read it somewhere." I examined the page, flipped forward, flipped back. The words I'd read were not there. Not anywhere. The page was about a different topic altogether. That passage...C. S. Lewis hadn't written it.

I had read it, though. Over and over. And now I believed it.

GIFT FROM THE SEA
by Mary McKheen

I was stressed out from my job as a social worker at a children's counseling center in Detroit. All day I'd been going through piles of paperwork—case after case of kids with heartbreaking stories. Like Jasmine, a six-year-old who'd recently lost her mother. I had an appointment with her later. Had I helped her at all in our previous sessions? My worries and stress had me pretty close to burning out. Take a break? Not with so much work to do.

Moving aside some papers, I spied a book in my desk drawer, *Gift from the Sea* by Anne Morrow Lindbergh. It had caught my eye at a used book sale. The front flap said it was about a woman's journey to find moments for rest and contemplation in her busy life. I sure could use some moments like that, I thought. But I had been so busy, I hadn't even found time to read it.

Now I gave it a quick glance. Each chapter began with a drawing of a seashell. The author described one shell, a snail shell, as resembling a resting kitten curled up in a ball. "Patience is what the sea teaches. Patience and faith. One should lie empty, open, choiceless as a beach—waiting for a gift from the sea," she wrote. A nice idea...but she wasn't a social worker. I can't just sit around and hope things work out; I've got too much to do.

I braced myself and opened the waiting-room door. There was Jasmine. She looked different from the last time I'd seen her. Her blonde ponytail swung and a smile was on her face, like she had something exciting to share.

"Miss Mary, I have a surprise for you!" she shouted when she saw me, rushing in and bouncing up and down on her toes.

She handed me a small cardboard box. "I found something this morning when I was playing in my backyard," she said. "I knew that I wanted to give it to you."

Something she had found in her backyard? I wondered. I carefully opened the box. I knelt down and hugged Jasmine. I couldn't let myself burn out. The message was clear. Inside was a gift from the sea, found far from it. A snail shell—just like the one in my book.

PICTURE YOURSELF ON A BEACH
by Lori Kegel Ellis

If only I could be there, I thought. *It's paradise.*

It was close enough to touch. A sparkling blue bay, dotted with sailboats. A cityscape in the distance, hugged by tree-covered hills. In the foreground a brick patio, where a table was set with two empty chairs beckoning me to come take a seat in the sun and enjoy the view.

Too bad it was only a painting on my dining room wall, tucked inside a weathered wooden window frame. Outside my *real* window was just your typical suburban neighborhood a half hour north of Seattle, where I'd lived for the past twenty-four years and raised my daughter, Kelsey. At least she was out in the world having adventures, living abroad in Warragul, Australia, for three months, doing an internship with the Rope Factory Church.

I'd just gotten a call from her. "Mom, I love it here," she said. "You'll love it too. You could use the break. I can't wait for you to visit!"

"Kels, I wouldn't do this for anyone else. You know I hate to fly." That was putting it mildly. I dreaded it. Too many bad experiences. And Australia was on the other side of the globe.

Then again, life in Washington hadn't exactly been easy lately, one reason I was happy Kelsey had gotten away for a while. First, my husband, Kelsey's dad, asked for a divorce after twenty-three years of marriage. Not long after, my mother landed in the hospital. I lost my beloved grandmother, and my father took a bad fall. One crisis after the next. I tried so hard to keep it all together—especially my faith—but the truth was, I'd never felt so alone, so lost.

Was it any wonder I wanted to jump through that fake window? Leave the real world behind and go someplace that seemed to call me?

After all, I hadn't really chosen that painting. It had chosen me, fifteen years earlier.

I'd spotted the whitewashed window frame sitting outside an antique store in Snohomish, Washington. Something made me take a second glance. Suddenly, I saw its potential. *All it needs is a picture that's perfectly to scale—so it looks like I'm gazing out the window.* I didn't even bother to haggle over the price. Finding that picture, though, wasn't as easy. I searched. Nothing was right.

A month later I was running errands when I realized I was near a frame shop. I ducked in, flipped through dozens of prints and posters. Too small, too big, not right. I wanted something beautiful and serene, something that would put me at peace. Without giving much thought to bigger problems the ruler of the cosmos might have on His hands, I said a quick prayer.

All at once, I saw it—a flash of color. The edge of a painting peeked out from the bottom shelf. I'd never seen one that was so inviting, so peaceful, that had such an effect on me. I had to have it. It fit the window frame almost perfectly.

I stared at that painting every day. After my husband's decision. After the call about my mother from the hospital. The day Kelsey hopped on the plane and left me alone. I missed her something fierce. Her phone calls helped, but they weren't enough.

Before we hung up from our call, Kelsey asked if I had any second thoughts about visiting. She'd had to do some persuading before she left, finally getting me to agree to go at the end of her internship, so I could fly home with her. I bought the most expensive ticket of my life, still dreading the twenty-two hours I'd have to spend in the air.

I looked up at that fake window again. Kelsey was right, I could use a *real* break. "Don't worry," I told her. "I'm packing my bags."

Not one but three nail-biting flights later, I was in Australia. I thought I would squeeze Kelsey to death. We celebrated at a restaurant called Doyle's on Watson's Bay, a harborside suburb just outside of Sydney.

"They have some of the best seafood around," she said.

We took our seats at a table along a sandy strip of beach. I looked out into the distance, at the city and the Sydney Harbor Bridge, and watched the boats bob on the water. For the first time in a year, an inexplicable feeling of peace settled over me. "I could sit here forever," I said to Kelsey.

"Take your picture?" the waitress offered.

"Of course!" I said. I wanted to remember this moment.

The rest of the trip flew by. Before I knew it, Kelsey and I were back home. Back to reality. The uncertainty. The worry. And yet more than ever the picture on my wall gave me an inexplicable sense of peace.

Eight months passed before I finally went through the photos from our trip. (I must have taken a thousand!) Shots of Kelsey and me on our hot-air-balloon ride over Melbourne. Us in front of the Sydney Opera House. That wonderful meal at Doyle's...

I squinted. That photo...I looked up and leaned in close to my fake window. The bay, the sailboats, the table for two—everything was there except for the bridge.

I called Kelsey into the room and pointed at the painting on the wall. "Doesn't this look identical to Watson's Bay? Except no bridge."

Kelsey smiled slyly and lifted up the wooden frame. The bridge was hidden underneath. The picture was a perfect fit after all.

ICING ON THE CAKE
by Gwen Grinstead

My husband, Bill, and I weren't expecting an evening to ourselves. It's a rarity, raising three kids. I'd just put a chocolate cake in the oven for after dinner when my sister dropped by, unannounced. "I'll watch the kids," she said. "You two enjoy a fun night out."

"What should we do?" I asked Bill. He picked up a newsletter from a Catholic charity we supported. "Well, there's a potluck tonight," he said. A church potluck? That wouldn't have been my first thought. And the church was an hour and a half away.

"We don't have anything to bring," I started to say, but then the oven timer dinged. "Sure we do," Bill said with a triumphant grin.

On the way we got lost. When we arrived at the church fellowship hall, two lonely casseroles were all that was left on the serving table. A man was heading out the door. He stopped and stared at the cake pan in my hands.

"What's that delicious smell?" he asked.

"Chocolate cake," I said. "But I guess we're too late."

"Goodness no, trust me, nobody's leaving," he said, ushering us in. He took the cake and chatted excitedly with the group. Two women ran to the kitchen and brought out plates heaped with lasagna and chicken Marsala, baked beans and Swedish meatballs. The man we met at the door took our drink orders. Everyone waited on us hand and foot, even the priest. It was too much. You'd think Bill was the Pope or something! When we finished eating, everyone lined up for my cake. They all cheered when it was unwrapped.

"Okay," I said. "What's going on?"

"It's truly a blessing that you're here tonight," the priest said. "You see, after dinner I offered a closing prayer, thanking God for the meal. It had just been missing one thing. I didn't want to sound ungrateful, but said to God, 'Still, a warm chocolate cake for dessert would have been nice.' A minute later in you walked."

99.5 FM

by Judi Dotson

8:20 AM. The vast, featureless plains of the Texas Panhandle stretched monotonously before me on both sides of Interstate 40. On a cold day like this, not even a jackrabbit was moving. The harsh morning sunlight hurt my eyes. Between yawns, I reached into my car's center console for my sunglasses and put them on, then thought better of it. The sunlight was probably helping me to keep awake.

Visiting family in California had been fun. But next time, we'd fly. My daughter was already asleep in the passenger seat. After twelve hours of driving the day before, and leaving our hotel in Albuquerque at sunrise, we were both exhausted. I glanced at the car's digital clock. *8:23 AM.* Another couple of hours to Amarillo, then five and a half to Tulsa.

Music. Maybe that will help. I turned the radio on. Nothing but static. I hit the Seek button. The numbers flipped all the way from 87.9 to 107.9. The radio was as barren as the landscape. Should have expected that, this far from any town. I pressed the *Seek* button again. And again. Just when I was about to give up, the dial stopped on 99.5.

8:25 AM. "This is the dawning of the Age of Aquarius, the Age of Aquarius... Aquarius... Aquarius." Wow! I loved that song! It perked me right up. Memories flooded back from the summer of 1969, living in San Francisco with my husband. Occasionally we'd go out to a nightclub where it was a tradition for couples to sashay down the stairs to the dance floor. A handsome young singer my husband and I met there often asked if he could join me for a dance, even for just a few steps.

8:29 AM. The song drifted away, and after a few moments of silence came the words of an old, familiar hymn: "I come to the garden alone while the dew is still on the roses...." That brought me back to childhood, growing up in the small town of Slick, Oklahoma, and the Sunday mornings I spent in a tiny Baptist church. I could almost see myself there, sitting with my family in a worn pew, wearing my finest white dress. I joined the choir at the age of ten and sang with them until I graduated from high school. I never dreamed back then that people would wear jeans to church someday. How times had changed....

8:35 AM. The hymn faded out and the voice of Bobby Vinton began to croon, "She wore blue velvet..." just like it used to from the jukebox at a small private club on the edge of Oklahoma City—public bars weren't legal there yet. I was eighteen, a freshman in business school, and I went there with my friends and my fiancé. "Blue Velvet" was a favorite of ours, and always brought us out onto the dance floor.

8:40 AM. There was a longer silence, nothing but a soft crackle, until once more, a tune I'd long forgotten began to play. "If you see my milk cow, send her right on home." It was George Strait, but in my mind, it sounded like my dad. When the Bob Wills version played on the radio, Dad always sang along. It was his favorite tune to break the silence on our long drives to visit relatives seventy miles away in Pawnee. I was only eight, but I remembered staring out the windows as we cruised along the highway, reading all the Burma-Shave billboards we passed by, feeling safe, feeling loved.

"Mom? What kind of station are you listening to?" Jen had woken up in the passenger seat. "They switch from gospel to country to sixties rock?" She snapped her seat upright and reached into the cooler for a bottle of orange juice.

"It's ninety-nine point five," I said. But Jen was right. There was something strange about the station format. I'd been so wrapped up in the music and the sweet memories that only then did I realize—there'd been no commercial breaks. No disc jockey. Just one favorite song after another, like some kind of soundtrack. *A soundtrack to my life.*

"I'll find some modern rock to wake us up," Jen said with a yawn. She reached for the *Seek* button.

But I was already wide awake. "Wait..." Too late. The radio searched through the dial, 87.9 to 107.9. Nothing. "Where are we that the radio has no stations?" Jen asked.

"Somewhere near the Texas-New Mexico border."

"More like the Twilight Zone," Jen responded.

After we got home, I couldn't put my curiosity to rest. What had been that station I'd found? I looked online, but couldn't find any 99.5 that played the variety of music I'd heard. Finally, I called the FCC. I told the man who answered exactly where we had been, and the frequency that had been displayed on the radio.

"I'm sorry, ma'am, but there is no station at ninety-nine point five in that listening area," he said. "Not even close."

I smiled. Wherever the signal had come from, I owed a lifetime of thanks to the deejay.

THE MOUSEHOLE ROAD CLUB
by Patricia Camp

We were all just sitting there in the car waiting for eight-year-old Christopher to make up his mind.

"Have you seen anyone you want to give those to?" I asked him for the umpteenth time, nodding at the bouquet of flowers he clutched in his hands.

"Not yet, Gramma," he said. "I'll know 'em when I see 'em."

Let's just hope he sees someone soon, I thought. We didn't have all day. I should explain that giving flowers to a stranger was one of our fun summer rituals. Every Wednesday we'd pile into my car and set off on an adventure. The Mousehole Road Club, we called ourselves. "Mousehole" came from a nickname my husband, William, had for a secret hideout where he'd played as a child. It fit our bunch perfectly! We'd have picnic lunches. We'd do "Get Lost Days" when the kids took turns telling me which direction to drive. And I would comply with (almost) unquestioning obedience. Other times we'd collect cans from the park and cash them in to save up for a wintertime trip.

Today's activity, "The Stranger Bouquet," was their hands-down favorite. I'd pick flowers from my garden and one grandchild would have a chance to determine a random recipient. Usually the kids chose quickly, even decisively. Not today. Chris kept stalling, searching.

"Hey! How 'bout that man walking down the sidewalk?" six-year-old Nick asked, squirming in the backseat.

"Or that lady in front of her house," nine-year-old Jennifer chimed in.

"Nope and nope," Chris said, shaking his head.

Exasperated, I finally said, "Chris, if you don't find someone soon, I'll give the bouquet to the next person I see."

"Wait!" he shouted. "The grocery store! We gotta go back there." We'd already passed by once. I shot Chris a look but he was so insistent I gave in. The grocery store was having a slow day. No one went in, no one came out. I pulled into the exit lane.

"There he is!" Chris shouted, pointing excitedly to a man leaving the fast-food restaurant next door. About time! I drove the car over and parked.

The man was impeccably dressed in a dark suit and tie. He was holding a cup of coffee, walking up to a shiny Cadillac. I didn't want to judge by appearance…but wasn't there someone, well, more in need of a Stranger Bouquet?

"Are you *sure* that's him?" I asked Chris. "He looks busy."

"Yes, Gramma," he said. No hesitation. He pushed open the door, jumped out, and hurried toward the man. "Sir! Sir, these are for you!" we heard him yell, holding out the bouquet.

The man kept walking. Chris caught up. The man stopped. I pulled closer and rolled down the window, thinking I might have to extricate my grandson from this situation.

"For me?" the man asked. "But why?"

"Well, this morning I asked God to tell me who to give them to," Chris explained. "You're the one."

The man's eyes welled up. He leaned down and wrapped his arms around Chris. I got out of the car, concerned.

"Sir, are you okay?" I asked.

He wiped his eyes. "Yes, it's just…I buried my son today. I just came from the cemetery."

"I'm so sorry," I said. He waved my comment off.

"I asked God to let me know that He was with me.…"

The kids all climbed out of the car then, and the man gave each of them a hug. I bowed my head and wiped my eyes. The Mousehole Road Club had struck again.

AN AMERICAN IN CHINA
by Rita Turner

Teach English in China and experience the nuances of an ancient culture....

I was experiencing the nuances, all right. I looked down at my bed—a generous description for that narrow plank two inches off the ground. Not even a thin mattress to rest my arthritic sixty-two-year-old American self on. My roommate, Rosemary, giggled. I was used to that by now.

I'd arrived in Bao'an, on the outskirts of the city of Shenzhen, three weeks earlier, excited to teach English as part of my master's degree program. I'd pictured my students hanging on my every word. It turned out eight-year-olds are the same everywhere—hyper! Plus, it was sweltering, and my classroom didn't have so much as a fan. Thank goodness I'd finally mastered my first Chinese sentence. *Wo yao bing shui*—I'd like ice water. The other teachers in the program were just out of college, up for anything. Even the chicken feet and beef-blood stew in the cafeteria. Me, I couldn't seem to settle in and get comfortable.

Especially on that board bed. I crouched and crawled onto it, my joints creaking. Rosemary laughed again. "Rita, why'd you decide to enroll in this program, anyway?"

I'd seen the puzzled looks from the other teachers. The locals who stopped and stared—and sometimes reached out to touch my white-blonde hair. What in the world was a sixty-something widow from Southern California doing in Bao'an, far off the tourist track?

I shifted to take the pressure off my bad knee. "Okay, Rosemary, if you really want to know...."

It all started with my husband, Paul. I never thought I'd find my soul mate at age fifty-two. Then I met Paul at a church luncheon. It was the beginning of a wonderful adventure. Which was really different for me.

I'd been at the same job—teaching elementary school—for thirty-nine years. Not like Paul. He'd sailed the seven seas, even lived in Japan. I'd never set foot on foreign soil. Paul made plans for us to travel, see the world. "Rita, you gotta dream big," he was always saying. "Get out of your comfort zone." We were going to drive cross-country. Backpack through Europe.

But five years into our marriage, Paul died of cancer. Counseling, support groups—nothing eased my grief. What was I supposed to do with my future now that the love of my life was gone?

Then, one spring morning, a voice blaring from my clock radio jolted me awake: "Teach English in China and experience the nuances of an ancient culture. . . ." Just as suddenly, the ad cut off, mid-message. The radio went back to music from the station I kept it tuned to. Strange.

I wanted to hear the rest of the message. I listened for that ad for a whole month. It never played again. Finally, I called the station.

"We don't air any commercial like that," the manager said. I persuaded her to send me a list of the station's sponsors. I e-mailed every name on the list, asking, "Do you offer a program to teach in China?"

Only one sponsor said yes—Concordia University. It was about to launch a pilot program for teaching English in China, as a requirement for its Master of Arts in International Studies degree. I met with the dean and the program director for an interview.

The dean looked at me the way the locals here did. "I was surprised to receive your application," he said. "How did you even hear about the program? We haven't officially launched it yet."

"On the radio." I explained about the ad.

The dean looked even more perplexed. He turned to the program director. "Did you place that ad?"

The director shook his head. "We don't have the budget for it."

Nobody could account for the voice that came from my radio. An odd message blaring in the darkness, one I couldn't ignore.

"So I packed my bags," I told Rosemary. "I needed to dream big. Leave my comfort zone and try someplace new." I tapped the plank beneath me. "I just wish it came with a more comfortable bed."

This time when Rosemary laughed, I did too.

FATEFUL FIFTY
by Adam Hunter

It was a fifty-dollar bill. Ulysses S. Grant on the front, "In God We Trust" on the back. As someone only a few years removed from college, I needed every buck I could get. But the bill remained folded in my wallet for months, untouched. Its worth was beyond monetary.

"This is too much, Pop," I'd said to Papa Morey, my grandfather, when he gave it to me. I was visiting him in New Jersey. Every weekend since Nana Rita passed away, a year earlier, I took the ferry across the Hudson from New York City to see him. We'd go out for breakfast or watch a Yankees game on TV. And talk, mostly about love. I rarely mentioned girls to my parents (I didn't want Mom planning any weddings prematurely), but Pop had just lost his one and only. Telling him about a girl I'd met lit up his face with joy.

"Is she Jewish?" he'd want to know. As an American Jew who'd helped liberate Holocaust survivors during World War II, that was important to him. "Is she pretty?" he always asked—that was equally important. "Smart? Funny?" came after that. And of course, was she a Yankees fan?

Pop had given me money before when I left to go home, but usually it was just cab fare. "I want you to use this to take out a girl," he said. "Not just any girl, a special girl. The one you're going to marry."

Who knew when I'd meet that girl? How would I know she was the right one?

A few weeks later, Pop suffered a stroke. He held on long enough to say good-bye to us, but he was ready. He was going to see Nana.

The next months were tough. When I did start dating again, it was with a heavy heart. *Pop will never get to meet this girl.* I went out, but didn't feel any sparks. My aunt suggested a blind date with a girl she thought would be perfect for me, so I gave her a call. "Um, I've been in a serious relationship for a year," she said. Yikes. So when my roommate's girlfriend wanted to set me up with a friend of hers, I refused. I'd had enough embarrassment.

Then one Saturday morning, my roommate and I decided to get some fresh air. On the street, we bumped into his girlfriend—and her friend. My roommate swore it was a chance encounter. I wouldn't have been mad even if they had orchestrated it. The four of us went for chips and salsa, but it felt like it was only the two of us. She'd just returned from ten months' working with disadvantaged communities in Israel. We talked about our families, keeping kosher when our friends didn't and, most important, the Yankees. "It's a good thing you're a fan or else I couldn't talk to you," she joked.

For our first real date, I picked an Italian restaurant in my neighborhood. I'd never been there, but it had little candlelit tables and a garden in back. The night went perfectly, from the way she laughed at my lame jokes to the way she picked gnocchi off my plate as if we'd been together for years. The staff even gave us a free dessert—crème brûlée, which had been Nana Rita's favorite.

Finally the bill came. "Cash only." *Uh-oh.* I opened my wallet. Just credit cards—and the fifty-dollar bill. The one intended for the girl I would marry. I looked across the table, and I was struck with an overwhelming feeling that I couldn't just run out to the ATM. I didn't know what the future held for us, but I'd never felt as sure of anything as I did right then.

I took the fifty out and laid it in the check holder. It exactly covered our meal, including the tip. The server came to take it away. And it was gone.

Three years later, I stood under the chuppah in my tux on my wedding day, watching that Jewish, beautiful, smart, funny girl walk up the aisle, the very girl my Pop knew I was destined to marry.

CHAPTER 2

Comfort Your Heart

NEXT STOP, HEAVEN
by Karen Krone

I can see Bill now. Running up to the train, excited at the journey ahead. The next big adventure. He's ready to take a trip with "the Great Conductor." For a moment, he hesitates. Smoke billows from the engine. A whistle blows, one long, mournful cry. Bill glances back. But the train is leaving and it's time to hop aboard that big red caboose to heaven. . . .

The words of the eulogy Bill's friend Larry had delivered were still on my mind when the huge Hummer limo pulled up to the ranch-style house on Estates Drive. Our former home, where we'd raised our boys. I couldn't help but wonder: What had Bill's journey really been like?

I tried to picture Bill healthy and free, as Larry had described in his eulogy. No longer bedridden. God greeting him with a locomotive and a shiny red caboose. Oh, how Bill would've loved that! For as long as I'd known him—since high school—he was crazy about model trains.

His parents had surprised him and his little brother with a brand-new train set one Easter morning, brightly painted eggs hidden in each of the boxcars. It wasn't until we were married, though, that I found out I'd be sharing my house with dozens of pre–World War II trains and endless feet of track. We hadn't been able to take a proper honeymoon because Bill had to teach class at Washington University. But the day after our wedding we paid a visit to the Museum of Transportation in St. Louis. Bill spent hours crouching beneath full-sized engines, asking questions and taking pictures. That's when I knew for sure—I'd married a train nut!

We planned several vacations around the National Train Collectors convention. We traveled from Illinois to Pennsylvania to Florida. Our three boys loved to brag that their dad was "the train guy." Their school classes took field trips to our basement train room, where Bill had laid out a complex labyrinth of tracks and towns, complete with miniature trees, benches and lampposts. A whole other world.

Bill was diagnosed with pancreatic cancer in 2009. I was devastated. I couldn't imagine life without Bill. And his trains.

The trains soon became more than a hobby. That other world became an escape. The minute we returned home from a chemo treatment, he'd go downstairs. He was at peace there, sitting at his workbench tinkering with engines. In those quiet moments, he was transported to a place where the pain was remote. Later, he was too weak to go up and down the stairs. I'd bring up a few old Lionel trains and set them out on a TV tray, so Bill could work on them in the family room.

Now that Bill was gone, the house was so quiet. I missed the hum of the trains going around the tracks. I'd always been able to hear that *clickety-clack* from the kitchen upstairs. I never realized how familiar and comforting that sound was—until now.

I wanted to do something different to celebrate Bill's life. We'd always been a no-frills kind of people. Never splurged on new cars, always bought dependable used models. But for the day of the funeral, I'd rented a twenty-five-seat, triple-axle Hummer limo to take our closest family and friends on a tour of all the places Bill loved most in our hometown. It wasn't a train, but it was the next best thing.

After the funeral service, and Larry's beautiful eulogy, we'd piled into the Hummer—all twenty-two of us, including our three sons, three daughters-in-law and eleven grandchildren. We put on the 1950s music Bill and I had listened to when we were dating and shared our favorite memories.

The first stop on the tour was Faith Salem Church, where Bill and I were married all those years ago. Then Bill's elementary school. His childhood home. Jennings High School, where we met. And, finally, our house on Estates Drive. We'd downsized after the boys moved out. What an ordeal, cleaning out the stuff we'd accumulated over the course of thirty-seven years. Even though we'd sold it six years before, it still felt like home.

"We should knock on the door and ask to go inside," my son Brad said.

Just then, a car pulled into the driveway. A man got out and walked briskly toward us.

"Did I win the Publishers Clearing House sweepstakes or something?" he asked, taking in the Hummer.

Brad explained.

"Why don't you come inside?" the man offered. "Take a look around." We followed him into the foyer.

"You're lucky," he said. "I came back because I forgot my briefcase. Listen, I'm glad I caught you. I have a gift for you."

He disappeared into the garage. What could it be? I doubted we'd left something behind. On moving day, we'd searched the house from top to bottom to make sure we hadn't forgotten anything.

The man came back with a large framed picture.

"I found this when we moved in," he said, turning it to show us. "My wife kept bugging me to throw it out, but for some reason I just couldn't."

A painting. A beautiful painting. It had once hung in Bill's train room. Something he'd found at a garage sale years ago. But that wasn't all.

The scene in the painting...a train with a red caboose, on its way out, chugging through a landscape unlike any on earth. Exactly the picture Larry had painted in Bill's eulogy, down to the smallest detail. And for an instant I heard the faint sound of a train whistle, echoing in the distance.

THE SHADOW BOX

by Janet Hall

A golf ball, a wind-up ornament, ladybug figures, a shiny penny—
to anyone else these were just an odd assortment of objects, a jumble
of twenty-one artifacts. But for me, each one held a vital connection to
my son. Sometimes they felt like the only connection.

I'd moved the collection around the house, never finding the right
spot. Now the pieces sat on my dresser, a few tipping over whenever I
pulled open a drawer. "I wish I had a good place to keep these," I said to
my husband, Jim, before we headed out to run some errands one day.

"Let's check the thrift store," Jim said. "Maybe we'll find something
there."

I didn't want to hide them away in a box. Since Matt's death from
heart failure, whenever I felt overwhelmed by grief the strangest thing
happened: I'd come across a reminder that he would always be with us.

I'd spied the golf ball lying in our side yard through the bathroom window one morning while I brushed my teeth. A gleaming white golf ball,
miles from any course! Matt was a golf nut. He'd even traveled to Scotland
to play. I hurried outside to scoop the ball up off the grass.

The shiny heads-up penny I'd picked up off the floor of the super-
market on my first outing after Matt's death. I felt like it was a penny from
heaven, a sign that I had to force myself to rejoin life.

The wind-up ornament was a gift from a friend. She found it in a craft
store. It played "This Little Light of Mine," one of Matt's favorite hymns,
a song we played at his memorial service. "It seemed meant for you," my
friend said.

One day over lunch I was talking about someone who had received
a ladybug as a sign that a loved one was safe in heaven. "Where's my

ladybug?" I asked. A woman at a nearby table overheard us. It turned out she had been with Matt when he died, and tried to revive him with CPR. When I got home, on my yellow kitchen tablecloth, I found a live ladybug waiting. Ever since, ladybug toys, pictures and carvings leaped out at me at every turn.

I stood up the pieces that had toppled over, balanced the ball against the ornament so it wouldn't roll off the dresser. It seemed silly to attach such importance to these things. Were they really God's way of comforting us? Or was it all in my head? A refusal to let go?

Jim and I dropped by the cleaners and the post office, then stopped at the thrift store. I browsed through the aisles for something to hold my Matt mementos. *What can display both a golf ball and a penny?* I thought, turning a corner.

My eye fell on a wooden shadow box. There were small, deep compartments of different shapes and sizes. I counted the spaces—exactly twenty-one—*perfect* to hold all my treasures. "Look, Jim!" I called, holding it up.

That was when I noticed the small plaque on the bottom of the frame. And the inscription, engraved in brass: *Matt's Collections.*

MY GOLFING PARTNER

by Ralph Aker

"Come on, Grandpa, come play golf with Mom and me," my grandson pleaded, pulling an extra set of clubs out of the closet.

I'd driven from Virginia to Missouri to spend time with my daughter and grandson, but golfing was the last thing I wanted to do.

"You two go on," I said.

My daughter put her hand on my shoulder. "What's wrong, Dad?" she asked. "You love golf."

It's true. I did love golf. But I just couldn't muster the slightest interest in playing these days.

For as long as I could remember, my lifelong friend Harold had been my golfing partner in Virginia. We were perfect together. I would hit a shot into the rough, and he would inevitably counter it with one that landed in the center of the fairway. It went like that for years, his shot always landing just a bit closer to the hole than mine.

Harold was more than a golfing buddy, though. We grew up together. He knew me better than almost anyone. But not long ago, cancer took Harold away from me. I missed him terribly. Golf would never be the same.

Still, the pleas of my daughter and grandson were too hard to refuse. "Okay," I said, "maybe just one round."

I stepped up to the tee at the Murder Rock Golf Course in Branson, Missouri, feeling a bit rusty. I pulled out the driver and took a swing. The ball arced high into the air...and plunked down in the tall crabgrass: ten feet off the fairway.

Ralph, you're not supposed to hit the ball in the rough, I could practically hear Harold playfully chiding me. Grumbling to myself, I went to retrieve the ball. I bent over to examine the lie.

Out of the corner of my eye, I saw another ball lying just a few feet away, almost on the fairway. I looked around. My daughter and grandson hadn't even teed off yet. No one else was playing through. Who abandons a perfectly good golf ball with a good lie? I wondered. I walked over, leaned down and picked it up.

That's when I saw the monogram stamped on the ball: H.D.R. The initials of my dear friend Harold Dean Roland. Still my golfing partner, and always will be.

DRAGONFLY SEASON
by Julie Stroh

The insects live underwater, wondering what exists above. One brave bug offers to climb the lily pad and report back. He makes his way up the stalk, breaks the surface and feels the sun's warmth. Suddenly, his body is transformed into a beautiful four-winged creature—a dragonfly. After soaring through the air, he tries to return home . . . but discovers he cannot dive beneath the water. He's unable to tell anyone about the wonders of the world above. . . .

The story wouldn't leave my mind. I pulled my jacket tighter against the late–October breeze, hurrying from my office to the drugstore, where I intended to buy a card. Occasionally I glanced up into the clear blue sky for those shimmering wings.

It was just a story, I thought. A parable about heaven in a book that a friend had put in my hands after my daughter's funeral, four months earlier.

Kari was only twenty-seven years old when she died in an ATV accident. She occupied my every waking thought. All it took was a simple "How are you?" from a coworker and I was lost. Or the sight of gerbera daisies, her favorite. Whenever the phone rang early in the morning, I remembered Kari, who always called me on her way to work. "Sunshine walking through the door" was how a friend described her, and that was spot on. When she died, the darkness took over.

I tried to remember every detail about her. The way her shoulders shook when she broke into that infectious laughter. The faint cherry-blossom scent of her body lotion—sometimes I used it just to feel closer to her. In the middle of the night, exhausted but unable to sleep, I sought refuge in my sewing room, stitching bib after bib for my grandkids, just as I had made pink dresses for Kari when she was little.

Take care of me, God, I prayed as I sewed. *I'm hurting so bad.*

Rounding the corner to the drugstore, I thought of the dragonfly pin Kari always wore on her winter coat. Gold with tiny amber rhinestones that twinkled in the light. Maybe that pin was one of the reasons the story stayed with me.

A few weeks after the funeral, Kari's husband, Donnie, came to visit. We'd put on forced smiles and tried to say the right things without losing it. We took a pontoon boat out on the lake, the lapping of the water filling the gaps in our conversation. Then I looked over at Donnie and gasped. A dragonfly with delicate blue wings was hovering just above his shoulder.

All summer, I saw dragonflies wherever I went, not just by the lake. In my backyard, a dragonfly landed lightly on my wrist. A swarm of dragonflies even surrounded my car on my drive home from work one evening. Every sighting of those slender bodies darting through the air felt like God had poked a needle through the darkness, letting Kari's light shine through.

Now it had been weeks since I'd seen one. Dragonflies couldn't survive the harsh Minnesota winter. The darkness returned.

Think of the good times, everyone kept telling me. *She wouldn't want to see you so sad.* How could I not be sad? I faced a gloomy winter, and the rest of my life, without my daughter.

I reached the drugstore and opened the door. A little bell chimed. The cashier glanced in my direction. That's when I froze, unable to take another step.

Everywhere I looked—the aisles, the displays, the discount bins and the card racks—translucent wings glimmered in the store's fluorescent light.

On wind chimes and garden stakes. Trinkets and souvenirs. Merchandise tagged for sale with one common theme: dragonflies.

"A late shipment of summer items," the cashier said.

They weren't late for me. The timing was perfect.

I felt myself emerging then, slowly breaking free. Out of the muddy waters below. Finally able to catch a clear glimpse of the sky above, where dragonflies go.

THE BLUE COAT
by *Carol Hahn*

A year after my husband, Keith, died, my family still felt lost without him. Of our three children, seven-year-old Matthew seemed the least equipped to deal with his shattered faith. For reasons I could not figure out, he became unusually attached to a blue coat I'd bought at a thrift store. North Texas winters are unpredictable, but even on warmer days, Matthew wrapped himself in it.

Then it disappeared. We checked his room, the closets, called his school. "It's gone, Mom," Matthew said. I wiped his tears and held him close. There was nothing I could do to console him. After losing his dad, even this small loss seemed unbearable.

We left Texas for Idaho, seeking a change. It wasn't for us. Six months later we moved to a Dallas suburb a good twenty miles from our old neighborhood. Even back home in Texas nothing felt familiar anymore without Keith.

Then, after Matthew's first day at his new elementary school, he came home with a smile I hadn't seen in a very long time. "Mom! Mom!" he shouted. "I found it! My blue coat!" He claimed it was on a shelf in his classroom.

"Sweetie, there are a lot of blue coats," I told Matthew. That coat had been lost more than a year before, miles away.

"I know it's mine," he insisted. "No one knows where it came from. I even asked the teacher."

"All right," I said, giving in. "Bring it home and we'll see."

The next day after school, Matthew pulled the coat out of his backpack. I could see how he had been confused. Anyone might have mistaken it for his old coat. The pockets were even a bit worn around the edges from some other boy plunging his hands in just as Matthew used to do.

I pulled down the tag to check the size. Written on it was a name. *Matthew.* In my handwriting.

TABLE FOR FIVE
by Suzanne Tranquille

Sunday brunch at the Farm Restaurant outside Old Forge, New York. Part of my family's ritual every summer, on our weeklong vacation in the Adirondacks. This year, though, the ritual felt empty. I waited for the harried hostess to find a table for four, my gaze ranging over the walls. Antique washboards, old-fashioned irons and tin milk jugs—Mother always got a kick out of the décor. The aroma of pancakes and sizzling sausages, the big, hearty, home-style breakfasts with names like the Lumberjack Special—it made me think of how Mother loved her eggs scrambled, with an English muffin. Our party of four? My seventy-seven-year-old father, my sister, our friend Christine—"the third daughter"—and me. Mother had died of a heart attack just five weeks earlier, ten days before her and Dad's golden anniversary.

At first Dad had refused to come: "I've never been on vacation without Elaine in fifty years, and I'm not going to start now." He was still struggling with his grief—we all were—but of course it was harder for him. Eventually, we persuaded him to join us.

The hostess returned, smiling and holding four menus. "There are no tables for four, but we do have a larger one set for five," she said. "I can seat you there right away."

I saw the sadness behind Dad's eyes. Even here we were being reminded of Mother's absence.

The day before, just after we'd arrived, I'd kicked back on the porch of our rented cabin overlooking the lake, as Mother loved to do. The late-afternoon sun glittered on the water like a thousand diamonds. That was one of the reasons we called the place Golden Pond, because the scene seemed to have been lifted right out of the classic movie. Four other cabins were nearby, each hidden by a thatch of tall pines. The perfect getaway, especially after Mother's first heart attack, nine years earlier. We thought we'd lost her then. This place was healing, restful, exactly what our family needed.

Sometimes deer came right up to us, and we fed them out of our hands. Friends came over and we enjoyed their company, uninterrupted by anything but the breeze rustling through the pines. Some days we'd go shopping in the pretty little town or drive along the lakes of the Fulton Chain. This year, though, I didn't feel like doing much.

There was a sudden movement in the woods. A big, furry dog, a husky, ambled toward me. A neighbor's dog, I supposed. His tags jingled around his throat.

I reached out, and the husky nuzzled my hand.

"Hello, boy," I murmured. He looked up at me with sad eyes. Did he sense my own sadness? "What's your name?" I asked, looking at his tags.

Shiva, the name tag read.

I knew enough about Jewish tradition to know what that word meant. The weeklong Jewish mourning period, after a loved one passes on. A time to grieve before returning to everyday life. The last five weeks had felt like that to us.

As quickly as he appeared, the husky turned and ambled away, vanishing into the trees.

I'd told Dad about it. It didn't seem to comfort him the way I'd hoped it would. *I've never been on vacation without Elaine in fifty years....* He hadn't said much more since we'd left home. We'd been given nine extra years with Mother, a blessing we were grateful for, but it still felt she'd been taken too soon.

Now the hostess led us through the maze of tables to the back of the restaurant, and I thought maybe Dad was right—this trip had been too soon as well. We reached the table for five, sunlit by the window. "Thank you," I said, and pulled out my chair, ready to take a seat.

Dad and I gasped at the same time. My sister and our friend saw it next. I looked from the table to Dad, to the table and back to Dad again. He was smiling.

Next to the sugar bowl, by the empty seat, illuminated in the sunlight, was a small white plastic sign, printed with a large black capital letter. *E.* To anyone else, just a table marker. To us, it stood for Elaine. For Mother.

We asked the waitress not to take away the fifth chair and place setting. The one meant to sit there wasn't too far away.

THE MISSING PHOTO
by Marilyn Sharrow

Dad loved a good cigar. He would walk around all day with one hanging from his mouth, looking like Groucho Marx. He had Groucho's sense of humor too, always quick with a joke or a prank. When he passed away, the stories friends and relatives told at the funeral highlighted how much of a character he was.

My favorite story? It happened on a trip with some of Dad's friends years ago, a four-hour drive from home. When they arrived at their destination, Dad discovered his half-chewed cigar on top of the rear bumper—he had left it there while packing up the trunk. "I was wondering where I'd put that," he said. Then, to everyone's horror, he stuck the cigar back into his mouth!

I chuckled at that one. But in the days after the funeral, as Dad's absence took hold, I found it a struggle to smile. I was in such a haze of grief, I couldn't seem to focus on anything.

One snowy winter morning, I stacked up the photographs of Dad that we'd displayed at his funeral, intending to take them over to my stepmother's place. I stared at one photo of Dad chewing on his cigar, happiness lighting up his face. *I wish I knew he was happy now*, I thought. I set the pictures down on the roof of my car while I loaded in a flower arrangement to take to Dad's grave.

I had so many errands that day, I never made it to my stepmother's. I was in bed that night when I bolted upright. I'd never put those photos in the car! I'd just driven off with them still on the roof. They were probably all over the road!

In a panic, I woke my husband. We got dressed and searched our street with a flashlight. Somehow, we located all of the photos but one.

The next morning we drove around the neighborhood, scanning the side of the main thoroughfare for that last missing picture. "Stop!" I said. "That's got to be it...."

We got out and checked. Sure enough, the glossy photo of Dad's happy face stared up at me from the cold, wet ground. Undamaged, incredibly. But it was something else that brought a smile to my face.

Pointing to the photo was a cigar—its end burned and ready to be chewed.

HIS EYE IS ON THE SPARROW
by Joy Dillman

Sparrows. A selfish, inconsiderate species, it seemed to me. Each morning I gazed out my kitchen window, binoculars in hand, hoping to glimpse the colorful songbirds for which the Texas Hill Country is famous. Bluebirds, goldfinches, hummingbirds, black-crested titmice, a dozen varieties more. Instead, I got sparrows, gangs of them, monopolizing the bird feeders. Ugly brown sparrows making giant messes of the seed—messes I had to clean up daily. *Good-for-nothings,* I thought, glaring at them one Wednesday morning.

It was later the same day that I learned that Jane, my best friend, disagreed strongly. "'His Eye Is on the Sparrow' is my favorite gospel song," she said. "I play it every night." She recited her favorite lyric—"I sing because I'm happy, / I sing because I'm free. / His eye is on the sparrow, / and I know He watches me"—and began humming the melody.

I sat next to Jane's bedside in an assisted-living facility, holding her hand and my tongue. Jane was dying of lung disease, bedridden and on oxygen. She was fifteen years older than me, but had never looked it until now. We'd met more than a decade earlier, working together at an education program for developmentally disabled children. She had made me a better teacher and in time became my closest confidant. Even after she retired, we remained good friends.

When she got sick, we began visiting for two hours every Wednesday. Maybe because we knew time was running out, we talked about everything. Our families. My challenges at work. Our beloved Dallas Cowboys. Elvis and Sinatra. And, most often, our faith. I prayed for her to recover, even though I knew it was hopeless. We both did.

Jane finished humming the hymn and squeezed my hand. "Joy, I want you to give the memorial address at my funeral," she said.

That was one thing I didn't want to talk about. I didn't want Jane talking about it either. Besides, wouldn't her children want to do it? Her grandchildren? But she persisted and I finally agreed.

"Be sure to play 'His Eye Is on the Sparrow,'" she said.

I promised and changed the subject.

We didn't speak again about funeral plans. Jane might have been ready to face her death, but I was not. I wanted her to hold on, to fight. I tried to keep the mood light throughout my next few visits, but Jane got worse. Her voice became raspy. It was painful for her to say more than a few words at a time. It hurt so much to see her this way, but it hurt more to think of losing her.

In four years I'd never missed a single one of our Wednesdays together, but when my parents asked me to visit them in Nashville, I thought I could use the trip to clear my head. I phoned Jane to tell her. She understood. "I'll miss you," she said.

On a sunny afternoon I took a walk in my parents' neighborhood, down a path lined with cottonwood and sumac trees. I hadn't gone far when I heard a furious rustling and a familiar tweeting. *Sounds like a sparrow,* I thought.

Looking up, I spotted the bird, a few feet above me in the branches of a big cottonwood tree. Flapping wildly, dangling from one leg, upside down. I squinted and saw that the leg was caught in the tendrils of a vine wrapped around a branch. The bird struggled mightily, trying to shake free. It failed. Again it flapped its wings, slower this time. It seemed near exhaustion.

I hated to see an animal suffer, even an insufferable sparrow. I reached up, but the limb was too high. I tried to snap the vine, but couldn't.

I raced home and woke my dad from an afternoon nap. He had five inches on me, and was a lot stronger. "I need your help," I said.

We ran back to the tree. The bird was still trapped, and was barely fighting now.

"Let me see what I can do," my dad said. He stood on his toes, gripped the branch and shook as hard as he could. All at once, the vine broke off and the sparrow took flight, rising quickly through the branches, disappearing into the sky.

I returned home to Texas the following morning to a ringing phone. Another of Jane's friends was on the line. "Jane died peacefully in her sleep at two o'clock yesterday afternoon," she said.

I closed my eyes and let the grief wash over me. I recalled how blue the sky looked through the branches of that cottonwood tree. How bright and promising. The suffering sparrow, set loose from the vine, flying up and away—at virtually the very moment Jane was set free too.

I looked out my kitchen window, writing Jane's tribute in my head. A family of sparrows alighted on one of my bird feeders, flicking seed everywhere. *Go ahead,* I thought, *stay for a while, enjoy my feeder. Then off you go, happy and free.*

STILL LIFE
by Deborah Walz

A doll. A handful of blocks. My two-year-old daughter's old baby shoe. I'd grabbed the items at random to bring to my art class, where I'd use them in a still life.

"Compose a scene," the teacher said, "then start painting."

I sat Raggedy Ann up with the shoe beside her. Now for the blocks. . . . I turned one a little to the left so I could see one letter and one number. Another had a picture of a cat facing out. Where I put things didn't really matter, it was just to have something to paint.

"Looks good," Sandy said. It was Sandy who'd gotten me into the art class—at a time when just leaving the house seemed impossible.

Four months into my second pregnancy, I'd miscarried. In one terrible night I lost my baby along with my confidence and hope. I had no energy, no appetite. I passed day after day in a haze. I no longer wanted to try for another baby. I couldn't endure another miscarriage.

Until then, Sandy was just my next-door neighbor, with three lively children. Her youngest boy was the same age as my daughter, Mary. Sandy helped her husband run a lawnmower and bicycle shop. She had her hands full, to say the least. But she became a lifesaver. She looked in on me every day. She watched Mary while I slept, washed dishes, did laundry. She taught me what it meant to be a good neighbor.

Sandy encouraged me to get out of the house. She signed us both up for the oil-painting class. "It starts this week," she said one afternoon. "I've bought all the supplies we need."

I didn't have the heart to say no.

Week by week, thanks to Sandy's enthusiasm and the teacher's patience, I'd come to love the class. For the first time since losing my baby I had something to look forward to.

So why did I choose baby things for my still life? I wondered now, uncapping my paints. I couldn't say. I just let my instincts take over and painted. I worked quickly and self-confidently, as if the haze that hung over me was clearing. Finally I sat back and admired my work. It looked like a scene from a nursery, the nursery that could have been. Strangely, it didn't make me feel sad. I was proud of my work. So were Sandy and my teacher.

The art class was like a door back to my life. Gradually my depression lifted. My fear of trying for another child didn't, though. One night I dreamed I was pregnant and woke up troubled. The next day I was having my wisdom teeth removed. When the anesthesiologist asked if there was a chance I was pregnant I said no. Two weeks later I found out I was going to have a baby—and I was terrified.

"What if the anesthesia hurt the baby and causes another miscarriage?" I asked my obstetrician.

"Just relax, and have trust," he said.

Trust. It was the one thing I hadn't gotten back in the two years since my miscarriage. I didn't trust my body. I didn't trust God. I lay awake at night imagining all the things that could go wrong. I tried to convince myself this was God's plan and not a mistake, prayed the baby would be healthy. But the fear never completely left me.

As my due date drew near, I got the nursery ready, hoping to chase away my fears. Searching a closet for some of Mary's old baby things, I came across a painting—my still life! I remembered with fondness the kindness of my friend Sandy and thanked God for her help through such a difficult time. I hung the painting above the crib. The colors matched the room perfectly.

At last I gave birth to Katherine Anne—happy and healthy. My husband, Marshal, and I brought her home, wrapped in a pink blanket. I laid her in the crib. Staring at my newborn girl, I felt nothing but joy.

Then I looked up at the still life, as if I were seeing it for the first time. There was the doll, next to a baby's shoe. At her feet was a block with an image of a little girl and the letters *K* and *A*—for Katherine Anne. It was between a block with *M* for Marshal and one with *D* for Deb. Another block showed a cat—like "Kat"—along with *O*, her blood type. Three more blocks showed a little clock set at 4:02, the time she was born, and the numbers 6, 1 and 7—June 1, 1977, my new daughter's birthday! She was born right on time.

The objects were anything but random. They'd been chosen with a careful hand by an Artist much greater than myself, with a vision I was only now beginning to see.

MOONLIGHT BECOMES YOU SO

by Nancy Portz

I could clearly remember those wonderful childhood days, even as my aging father's power of memory faded—happy days growing up with my four brothers and three sisters in that big rambling house we loved so much at 244 Robinson Street.

Who could forget those giddy, lively family dinners when all ten of us would crowd in around the table at dinnertime, times when Mom and Dad were known to spontaneously burst into song? "Moonlight becomes you so…," my dad would croon to Mom, doing his best Bing Crosby impression for us.

During the last five years of his life, Alzheimer's cruelly stole my dad's memory, until he could no longer remember any of his eight children, his wife of fifty-two years, not one of those special moments we had shared around the dining room table at 244 Robinson Street.

When Dad finally passed away, I tried to console myself by imagining him up in heaven, healthy once more, singing and doing his best Crosby imitations.

The whole family gathered at my house right after Dad's funeral. All of those sad faces, all of those tears, just compounded my own grief.

I wandered into the kitchen to get away from everything for a minute. There was a clock radio sitting out on the counter. Maybe some music will cheer me up, I thought. I flipped on the radio, sure that only a miracle could make me feel even the slightest bit better.

Right then, a song began playing. Not just any song. "Moonlight becomes you so," Bing Crosby sang.

I raced into the other room to grab my mom, my sisters and brothers. "You have to come in here," I said. "You'll never believe what I'm listening to."

They followed me into the kitchen and we all stood there together, listening. For the first time in weeks, I saw a smile on my mom's face.

"How often do you hear that Bing Crosby song on the radio?" I asked her.

Mom just shook her head.

Then I looked at the time on the clock face: 2:44 PM it read. 244 Robinson Street.

The clock remained that way throughout the entire song—all three minutes of it—before changing.

CHAPTER 3

God Delivers and Rescues

FIREPROOF
by Paul Archambault

"The road is impassable," the fire chief warned us. "You'll never make it." We'd pulled up next to his firefighting team in a snow of ashes, staring at Highway 39, the only route into the San Gabriel Canyon of Angeles National Forest, thirty miles northeast of Los Angeles. Thick smoke and bright orange flames roared from the trees beyond. My partner John and I, deputies for the LA Sheriff's Department, exchanged glances. "We've got no choice," I muttered. I wheeled our SUV around the roadblock, into the jaws of the fiery beast.

The firefighters had their job to do. We had ours: to save seventy-year-old Sigrid Hopson. She lived in a remote cabin in the woods and had stubbornly refused to evacuate. Refused, that is, until the massive forest fire reached her house. She'd placed a frantic call, begging for help. John and I both knew her. We couldn't leave her there.

We peered through the soot on the windshield, picking our way through plumes of black smoke and flames that danced across the road. "Watch out!" John shouted. I swerved to avoid a chunk of burning tree that exploded in front of us. The SUV's air conditioner was on full blast, but still the crackling heat singed the hair on my arms. I pulled on work gloves so the steering wheel wouldn't burn my hands.

The stench of burning rubber, plastic and paint filled the cab. "My God," John gasped, "the dashboard's starting to melt!" The next instant, the engine stuttered, starved of oxygen. I kept nursing the accelerator. Somehow we chugged on.

Then we reached "the Narrows." The road became one lane, with a granite wall on one side and a three hundred-foot drop on the other. At the bend of the road stood a stark reminder of how dangerous this stretch was even in normal conditions—a five-foot-high white cross, a memorial for someone who had veered over the edge. It wasn't hard to do.

I eyed the smoke and flames rising from the canyon. Any minute now, we wouldn't be able to pass. We'd be trapped. The firefighters' warnings echoed in my ears. *Last chance to turn around.*

The cross made me think of Mrs. Hopson. I couldn't let her become another memorial. We'd have to risk it.

Sweat streamed down our faces. Sparks blew across the fiery sky. We could barely breathe. Finally we reached a little parking area and spotted the goat path that led to Mrs. Hopson's cabin. "Wish me luck," John said, jumping out. He disappeared into the smoke. Moments later, a flaming tsunami rolled across the road ahead. We were as good as trapped.

I radioed our command post at the base of the canyon. "The fire's surrounded us. Send a helicopter. Or a water-dropping plane to clear a path...."

"Can't," came the commander's crackly voice. "Updrafts are too strong. Flying in isn't possible."

Then the radio died.

Where's John? I wondered, fighting off the thought that I was the only one alive up here. Could he even see? Breathe? The ground itself was aflame! I was ready to jump into the firestorm and find him. You never abandon your partner. All at once, a movement on the trail caught my eye. John appeared through the smoke, carrying a frail, frightened, white-haired lady—Mrs. Hopson. He put her in the rear seat, and dove in front. "Let's go," he said, choking.

I turned around quickly and headed into the deadly smoke. It was our only chance, and not much of one at that. I could barely see the road. What would happen when we reached that three hundred-foot drop?

Near the Narrows, the smoke enveloped us completely. I inched the SUV forward into darkness, waiting for that sickening moment when I'd feel the tires slip and we'd plunge off the edge. Would anyone even know how we died?

Then, suddenly, the billowing clouds of smoke parted. A blinding light filled the vehicle. Were we burning up? I recognized a shape, glowing fluorescent white in front of us, as if illuminated from within, like a beacon. The cross! Flames licked at shrubs around its base, yet it wasn't burning. *I'm here to protect you,* it seemed to say.

Guided by the glow of the cross, we rolled safely through the Narrows and on down Highway 39. Close to the bottom, the tires melted completely. We emerged from the worst of the smoke and coasted to a stop—just yards from the roadblock. The firefighters looked shocked. "We were sure you were dead," the chief said, while his crew attended to Mrs. Hopson.

"It was like someone was watching over us," I told John later as we gulped down water. Neither of us could figure out how that wooden cross was still standing while everything around it burned. Or how our half-melted SUV had even made it out.

"We *should* be dead," John said, shaking his head.

The fire burned for thirteen days, torching twenty-one thousand acres. After it was extinguished, John and I drove back up the mountain, in a new SUV, to see if Mrs. Hopson's place had survived. The forest along the way was nothing but ash. The cross at the Narrows was singed but somehow still standing.

Finally we reached the start of the goat trail winding between the charred skeletons of trees. John and I climbed out. The trail itself was indistinguishable from the rest of the black, scorched earth, save for a line of tiny patches of healthy green grass, evenly spaced, leading from the old woman's cabin. John's footprints, where he had carried Mrs. Hopson to safety.

CLOSE CALL

by Joyce Stark

In northeast Scotland, where I live, the Gulf Stream brings warmth to what would otherwise be a frigid climate—but it can also cause high winds. One day the weather service reported gusts topping one hundred miles an hour. I almost blew away when I left for work that morning.

Fortunately, I would be spending most of my day inside at my new job assisting John, a mortgage and financial services broker. I sat at my desk, looking out the large front window, awed by the sheer power of Mother Nature. Were the brick chimneys of the old houses around us actually swaying? Historic Flemish buildings from the eighteenth century lined our street, and our office was a "gable ender," a one-story house down a long alleyway surrounded by taller residences.

"I don't like the way that old chimney is moving about," John said. So my eyes weren't playing tricks on me.

"I'm sure it's nothing," I said. "These places have outlasted centuries of winds worse than this."

John disappeared around the corner into our tiny kitchen. I picked up my pen and got to work, entering appointments into his desk diary.

"Joyce?" I heard John call.

"Yes?" I said. There was no response.

I got up and walked down the hall to see what he wanted. Just as I turned into the kitchen...Boom! Smash! I heard the most deafening crash. It felt like the whole building was going to collapse around us. John and I huddled against the wall. Finally the rumbling stopped. We gathered up the courage and made our way to the front of the office.

The chimney stack of the building across the alley had tumbled down and smashed through the window by my desk. Shattered glass everywhere, bricks strewn across the desktop. I moved one of the bricks. Underneath was a black smudge on the desk—where the pen I'd been using had been flattened. John and I stood in shock.

I broke the silence. "John, I don't know what to say. If you hadn't called me, I would have been hurt."

John stared at me, confused. "But I didn't call you. It was a surprise when you came into the kitchen."

Surprise wasn't quite the word I would use.

NO ONE TO SAVE THEM

by James Nelson

Like any father, I was concerned for my daughter's safety. During college, Lori moved to a remote area outside Spokane with her horses and dogs, to a rustic cabin amid hayfields and pine forests, a mile and a half from her nearest neighbor. The vista from her home was achingly beautiful. But she was so isolated. I called a lot to check on her. "What if something happens?" I asked. "If you need help, there's no one around."

Lori laughed me off. "Oh, Dad," she said. "I'm fine."

I wanted to believe her. But every night I'd think about the coyotes out there in the woods, or of some unsavory characters she'd once seen around her cabin. "Dad, I'm okay," she assured me. "Clancy barks if he sees strangers. We can handle ourselves."

Still, I worried. When I worry, I pray. *God, my daughter thinks her black lab keeps her safe. Protect her, Lord, when he can't.*

One day, Lori called. Her voice didn't sound quite the same. "I have something to tell you," she said. "I don't want you to worry." As if that were possible. "I think you should know." I grabbed a chair and sat down.

A spring rain had been pelting her cabin all day, she said. She'd crawled into comfy clothes and snuggled on the couch with a good book and a cup of tea. But Clancy got restless. A bit of canine cabin fever. He needed exercise.

Finally, in the afternoon, the rain stopped. Lori laced up her heavy boots and pulled on a down jacket. "Come on, Clancy," she called.

Lori opened the door and Clancy nosed past her outside. He loped down the road toward Dead Man's Creek, about a third of a mile away. He knew the way. He swam the creek all the time while Lori watched from the one-lane bridge above.

The road was empty. They were almost to the creek, she said, when ominous black clouds rolled in. "I knew what that meant," she told me. The sky began spitting rain. She called to Clancy.

But he had other ideas. He had reached the embankment. "Clancy, no!" Lori yelled.

There was no stopping him. Labs are like that when it comes to water. He leaped into the creek.

Lori yelled for Clancy to come back. The rain and snowmelt had turned the shallow, slow-moving creek into a raging torrent. Clancy was nowhere in sight. Lori ran to the middle of the bridge and yelled his name.

Then she heard whimpers and cries. She spotted Clancy downstream. Normally a powerful swimmer, he struggled to keep his head above water.

The barbed-wire fence! There was pastureland on either side of the creek, and the owner had strung a line of fencing the length of his property, crossing the creek. Usually it hung two or three feet above the waterline. Clancy would swim right under it. But now, with the water so high, the fence was hidden beneath the surface. Clancy was snared on the barbed wire.

"Dad, I had to save him," Lori said.

She hit the water and used her sleeve to grab the fence, figuring she'd pull herself to Clancy. But the weight of her boots and jacket, and the force of the current, nearly dragged her under. By the time she reached Clancy, she was neck deep. The barbed wire dug into her jacket. She couldn't work herself free. Clancy kept going under, losing stamina. Running out of time.

"I grabbed Clancy around his chest and lifted him so his head was above water," Lori said. Every movement sank the barbs deeper into the dog's flesh. There was pain in his whimpers, fear in his eyes.

The creek was freezing, sapping her strength. In a few minutes she'd have a terrible decision to make: let go of Clancy or risk drowning.

She trained her eyes on the bridge, her only chance for rescue. Not a vehicle in sight. "Dad, I kept thinking of you worrying about me and praying." She looked to the sky and said a word of prayer herself.

She glanced back to the road. There was a pickup truck, the first car she'd seen since she and Clancy had set out. The truck crested the bridge. She yelled as loud as she could. But the truck continued down the road.

"I knew it was a long shot," she said. How would the driver have seen her? In this weather, he was concentrating on the road. As for hearing her yells—his windows were up, the rain was blowing and he was probably listening to weather updates on the radio.

Exactly what I was afraid of. No one out there to look after her.

She must have been heartbroken, saying good-bye to her beloved dog. All the times he had protected her! "I'm so sorry about Clancy...," I said.

"Dad, listen," Lori said. "I looked back to the road. The pickup. It stopped. And then backed up, onto the bridge."

Two men piled out. "Hang on! We're coming!" one of them shouted. They climbed down the embankment, worked Clancy and Lori free and pulled them from the water.

"I'm not going to stop worrying," I told her. "And I'm not going to quit praying."

"I hope you never do," Lori said. And then she told me the rest.

The men hustled her and Clancy into the truck to warm up. "Are you ever lucky!" the driver told her, as he drove them back to her cabin.

"I know," Lori said. "Thank you."

"No, it's not that. See, we never take this road," the driver said. "It's out of our way. For some reason, today we took this route to town. I can't explain it. I just got this weird sense about it."

AN AMAZING BRACE

by Ramona Scarborough

My family was driving across Canada to Montreal where my husband, Ray, and I were going to be helping out a new church. Ray had gotten a head start with our daughter in a rental truck stuffed with our belongings. I took my two-year-old, John, in our family car, a hardtop convertible jam-packed from floor to ceiling with piles of books to use in our work. They hadn't been able to fit in the truck.

We crossed into Ontario, driving along a narrow two-lane road. A heavy rain fell. Suddenly a truck veered into our lane. I turned the wheel sharply. The brakes screamed. Our tires hit the gravel on the shoulder. We went spinning off the road. *We're going to die,* I thought as the car flipped and rolled into a deep ditch.

Coming to my senses, I heard a man's voice from somewhere outside my car. "There's nobody alive in there." Everything was hazy; fine pieces of glass covered me from head to toe. The metal frame of our vehicle pressed tight against my back. I could barely breathe. John! Panicked, I reached behind me.

"Are you all right, honey?"

"Yes, Mama."

I craned my neck toward the window. "We're alive," I cried. "My little boy and I. Please help us!" A man reached through a shattered window and pulled John out. A few others pried the metal frame away enough for me to escape. Except for some minor scrapes, cuts, and bruises, we were okay.

A kind policeman escorted us as we rode in an ambulance to the hospital. He offered to take us to the impound lot to retrieve our belongings when we were ready.

Four days later we went to the lot. The insurance agent who accompanied us gasped when he saw the wreck. So did I. The policeman looked baffled.

"These hardtop convertibles don't have a window post to keep the roof up if they flip," he said.

"Then why weren't we..." My voice trailed off.

Our eyes turned toward the back seat. The roof had stayed up just enough so we weren't crushed, supported by an amazing brace. Piled from the floor to the ceiling were the books that hadn't fit in our rental truck.

Our Bibles.

FROM THE DEPTHS
by Logan Eliasen

They didn't think I could hear them but I could. Every word.

"He's deadweight," one voice said. "Exhausted, oxygen deprived, dehydrated. He's got nothing left."

"I don't know how we'll get him out before the rain comes," another man replied. "God help him if that tunnel floods...."

The cold cavern walls stung my cheeks. My lips were caked with dirt, dry and cracked. My empty stomach growled. I strained every muscle in my body, twisted left and right, exhaled every cubic inch of air that I could. It made no difference. I was trapped face down in a narrow shaft, far beneath the surface of Maquoketa Caves State Park. The words of the rescue workers in another chamber of the cavern echoed loud and clear. *If the tunnel floods...*

"Hey, Logan!" This voice was nearer. A female firefighter, one of the only rescuers small enough to squeeze in close to me. "You're going to be alone for a little bit while we switch shifts. You just take it easy. Okay?"

I lifted my head off the ground and craned my neck toward her. "Yeah, okay," I said weakly. The firefighter's flashlight disappeared around the bend and darkness poured into the shaft the way rainwater would, if the forecast held. These tunnels had been formed by the runoff from centuries of storms. What did drowning feel like? I imagined a steady stream trickling into the tunnel, rising around my face, filling my mouth and nose, flooding my lungs.

This was not the day I had thought I'd die. I'd just finished my sophomore year at Wheaton College, and my friends and I had decided that a spelunking trip would be the perfect way to celebrate. I knew these caves;

I'd explored nearly all of them with my father, starting when I was ten years old. I never dreamed I'd be in any danger.

Why hadn't I stayed at camp with the rest of the group? I could be setting up the tent, eating s'mores. But my friend Emma and I wanted to explore a real belly-crawler: Wye Cave. You enter through a sinkhole at the bottom of a valley and descend straight down to a steep boulder slope strewn with wood and leaves swept there by past storms. At the bottom is a tight pinch, about a foot high. You squeeze through, then the cave branches off into several smaller tunnels.

Emma was the first to get stuck. Two other cavers heard our shouts and sent help. It took five hours for firefighters to get her free. As we followed the rescuers out, snaking through the shaft, I got stuck myself. I'm over six feet tall, and an outcropping I'd tried to squeeze under trapped my chest against the tunnel wall. "You're okay, bud," one of them told me, examining the surrounding rock with his flashlight. "We'll lead her out and come back for you. Ten minutes, tops."

I'd believed it at the time. *They'll get me out, ten minutes, tops.* When they returned, they tried everything—harnesses and pulleys and ropes, chisels and drills—careful to avoid triggering a collapse. But all the twisting and jostling had moved me less than a foot. In fact, I was wedged even tighter, my hips pegged against the limestone. First ten minutes, then an hour, another hour. Now it had been twenty, nearly a day in the dark underground.

I wiggled my fingers, the only part of my body I could move freely. I couldn't feel anything below my knees—just pins and needles. I closed my eyes and breathed deeply from the oxygen mask the rescue workers had set up for me. I thought of my parents, waiting for me at the command center on the surface. They were praying, I knew. Losing their son couldn't be God's plan. But what if it was?

A memory flashed before my eyes. The morning before I left for the caves. I'd spent it deep-cleaning my bedroom. Washing my laundry, scrubbing the hardwood floors, organizing my drawers. I browsed the birthday and Christmas cards I'd collected over the years. I even found some of my old toys in the back of my closet and gave them to my three youngest brothers. I laughed at how excited they were about my yo-yos and Matchbox cars.

Somewhere deep down, had I known that I wasn't coming back from this trip? Had that been God's way of letting me get my affairs in order?

"Lord, let me free!" I shouted out into the darkness. I gave it my all, what little I had left. Pain shot through my body. I arched my back, twisted my arms and flailed my senseless legs. I clawed at the smooth stone until my fingers felt raw, and screamed like a madman. Didn't budge an inch. Too weak. My muscles withered.

It had gotten colder. The limestone walls wept with condensation. The rain would be coming soon—no rescue team could stop it. *This really is it. I'm twenty years old. This is the way I go.* I would never see my family again. Never finish college or buy my first car, never fall in love and get married. I pressed my face against the damp stone and sobbed.

God, I don't have anything left, I prayed one last time. *If there was any chance that I could free myself, it's gone. I need You now.*

I braced my hands against the rock wall and pushed. No strength at all. But cool air whooshed in around me. Like the rock itself had exhaled a breath. The pressure pinning my hips lifted.

I shifted my hips. This time, my muscles didn't burn. My body didn't struggle against the stone. Instead, it slipped around the crags, like water through a channel. I could hardly feel my body moving, but every part went exactly where it needed to go, with precisely the right amount of force. I'd imagined how my body needed to move dozens of times—now every motion was masterfully orchestrated and carried out, with a sudden forceful jolt. Was someone pushing me from behind?

I flopped out onto the ledge and collapsed like a broken marionette. I was free.

My body buzzed, the blood rushing back into my extremities. I looked behind me. No one there to have pushed me. I was quaking. Exhausted and sore. Someone had left a bottle of water and I guzzled it down. Ahead, beams of light danced around the dark cavern, the new shift of rescuers on their way.

Strong arms gripped me and helped me stand. Jubilant voices echoed off the cavern walls. "He's okay! He's free! Call command. We're bringing him up now."

I squinted against the bright afternoon sun. The rain had held off. The clouds were moving away. Dozens of rescue workers surrounded the mouth of the cave, cheering. My parents ran up to me, tears in their eyes. EMTs lifted me onto a stretcher and into the back of an ambulance.

It had taken all of their efforts to keep me safe, to keep me alive while I struggled down in the depths. But only a stronger push could set me free.

THE SURVIVORS
by John Senka

Welcome, US Army 4th Battalion, 9th Infantry, 25th Division. I stared at the sign outside the reception. For forty years I'd avoided these Vietnam vets' reunions. I didn't want to talk about the battle that haunted my nightmares, or how I'd survived.

The Battle of Mole City, December 22, 1968. We were a unit of five hundred American soldiers, stationed in deep bunkers along one of the North Vietnamese Army's busiest supply routes. I was twenty. Fit, strong, tough. My three months in 'Nam hadn't been much different than working on our family farm. I spent most days in the hot sun, digging the trenches the base was named for.

There was a holiday truce. After dinner, we opened packages from home with cards, cookies, and miniature trees. It almost felt like Christmas. At 10:00 PM we received our orders for the night: patrol, LP (the listening post), or perimeter. I was assigned to defend the perimeter.

All was quiet till midnight. The LP reported some NVA movement. The four of us in our bunker took our positions. Suddenly the night sky lit up. Flares. Mortar fire. A surprise attack!

We returned fire. There was a tremendous explosion. An anguished scream from the soldier next to me. I looked over. He was dead. I was struck too, in my right leg. Another grunt dove out the back of the bunker. I crawled after him.

We squeezed into the next bunker, filled with GIs. Something thudded into the mud. Another grenade! I threw myself as far from it as I could.

Boom! Blood ran from my ears. A third grenade rolled in. Shrapnel ripped into my belly. My rifle was clogged with mud. My injured leg was useless. We were overrun. Guys were falling, crying out for their mothers.

One brave sergeant climbed out of the bunker, firing his M16. His silhouette crumpled; his body rolled down past me. All I could do was lie there and wait for death.

I wouldn't have called myself religious, even though I wore a miraculous medal with my dog tags. Still, I shouted above the gunfire, "God, help me!"

Everything went silent. No explosions. No screams. Like I'd gone deaf. At the same time, I felt something hover over me. It fell softly upon my shoulders, warm, comforting, like I was a child being tucked into bed. Before I could figure out what it was, I blacked out.

When I came to, it was daylight. I moved to uncover myself, but nothing was there. Feet shuffled outside the bunker. Who had won? The NVA? Would I be taken prisoner? I pulled away a sandbag blocking my view. It thumped to the ground.

A helmeted head poked in. A US Army sergeant. "It's okay, soldier," he said.

I was the only one found alive in that bunker. The Army sent me home. The physical wounds healed. My other wounds didn't. Counselors told me that the nightmares were my mind trying to piece together what had happened in Mole City. Even after I learned that we'd been stormed by 1,500 NVA, outnumbered three to one, the survivor's guilt remained. Why had I been wrapped in that cocoon of safety, while others died?

For forty years, that guilt kept me away from reunions. I wasn't sure why I'd come now. But I took a deep breath and entered the reception hall. I put on my name tag and scanned the room.

A man came up, saw my name tag. "You're the guy I've been looking for."

"I'm sorry," I said. "Who are you?"

"Bob Chavous." He shook my hand. "I heard you were in the perimeter bunker near where I was supposed to be. I survived, the other guys didn't. It's not easy to talk about."

I understood all too well. Bob said he'd been assigned to the LP that night, one of the men who called in the warning about the enemy soldiers.

"Before we could withdraw, the sky lit up with a hundred mortars. We were pinned down in a rice paddy," Bob said. "I made my peace with God, and prayed He'd let my family know that I loved them."

He paused for a moment, searching for the right words. "Then it was like...a blanket settled over me and put me to sleep until the fighting was over."

A blanket of protection. I'd never know why it had covered me. But I hadn't been the only one. How many others at this reunion had felt the same thing? Been touched by the same inexplicable warmth that we told ourselves couldn't possibly be real?

I was ready to talk then. Ready to tell everything I'd held inside. I wasn't alone. Bob needed to know he wasn't either.

THE CASE OF THE MISSING CELL PHONE

by Robert Steinruck

Cell phones can be a pain in the neck. Whenever I seem to need mine, I can never find it. And this was one of those times, standing by my SUV shivering and wet.

It was whitetail hunting season—a day my three buddies and I had been anticipating for months. We parked our SUVs on a private rural lot just after dawn and hiked two miles—lugging rifles and backpacks filled with food, water, flashlights, extra clothing, two-way radios and, yes, cell phones—into the Pennsylvania State Game Lands wilderness. The weather was overcast and chilly, but we were determined to get us some deer.

We weren't in the woods but an hour before we lost our will for the hunt. The wind started, and then the rain. Oh, did it pour!

The four of us huddled like soaked dogs under a stand of hemlocks before we gave up and slogged an hour back down the now-muddy mountain we had climbed.

Now, hunching under the raised hatch of my SUV, I stripped off my wet clothing and quickly changed into dry clothes. From force of habit I reached into my backpack for my cell phone. I felt around. Nothing there. I checked and double-checked.

I knew that I had packed it before we headed out. Somehow, the phone must have fallen out of my bag at the spot where we had hunkered down in the woods, near the hemlock trees.

"I have two options," I told my friends. "One, I can forget the phone. Even if I hiked back to the stand of hemlocks and found it, it would probably be ruined by now. But I'm a stubborn guy. I can hike back up the mountain, in this pouring rain, and scrounge around in the brush trying to find it. I'm leaning toward option two."

My friend Bill thought I was crazy but insisted for safety's sake that he come along.

Back up the mountain Bill and I went. What had been a rocky path was now a muddy stream. Rain pelted us. Our feet slipped.

"You know," Bill said, "this isn't the brightest thing we've ever done."

At last we reached the hemlocks. We looked everywhere. No phone.

Light was fading. Time to give up and head home. Down the mountain we went, the only sound the squishing of our boots in the mud.

Then from somewhere I thought I heard a voice. I immediately turned to Bill. "Did you hear someone?" I asked.

"No," he said, keeping his head down, trying not to slip.

I heard the sound again.

"Bill?" I said.

"Yeah, I heard something," he admitted. It sounded like it came from somewhere up the mountain. We peered through the trees and the rain.

"There!" I said. "Up on that ridge!"

Bill's eyes followed where I was pointing.

A man was up there, waving his arms frantically. He was headed toward us, slipping and sliding. "Help!" he yelled. "Please help!"

We stood there. What kind of nut would be out here in the rain—well, other than us?

The man eventually reached us. He looked to be in his mid-twenties. "Please help me," he said, panting. "I came up here with a friend. I can't find him, and I don't know how to get back to where we parked." He told us his name was Tim.

I looked the young man up and down. His clothes were soaking wet. Not insulated or waterproof. Totally inadequate. He had an empty Thermos. No food. He had a cell phone, but it was dead.

"Come with us. We'll get you out of here," I said.

The three of us started down the trail, Bill and I helping him as best we could.

"Are you sure we're going the right way?" Tim asked.

"Just trust us," I said.

It was clear that Tim was disoriented. He couldn't even tell us his friend's name. We tried to keep him talking, so that he wouldn't pass out on the trail.

By the time we reached my SUV about forty-five minutes later, Tim was shivering uncontrollably. We helped him into the backseat. Bill gave him some almonds from his snack pack and coffee from his Thermos. I started the car, cranked the heat up and we wrapped him in a dry blanket.

Tim mentioned a general store he and his friend had passed on their way to the wilderness. I knew where it was. On the way there, a vehicle pulled up behind us and flashed his lights. For a second, I thought it was the cops. The driver got out. I rolled down the window.

"Are you Tim?" he asked.

I pointed to the backseat. "That's Tim," I said.

The driver said he had Tim's friend in his truck. He'd found him in about the same condition that we found Tim.

Tim stumbled out of my SUV and into the truck. Bill and I drove on home. On the way, we had a serious talk.

"Do you know the danger he was in?" I asked. "What would have happened if we hadn't been up there and he hadn't heard our voices?"

And then it hit us both—we would never have been up there to rescue him if not for my silly phone.

"I guess there was a good reason I lost it after all," I said. Together we offered a prayer of thanks.

But I hadn't lost it. Back home I finished unloading my backpack. That cell phone was right where I had put it.

INVISIBLE

by Renee Coy

Thirty-nine years. That's how long it's been since the day I stared absolute evil in the face—and it stared right through me. Like I wasn't even there.

I remember every detail. A stifling Saturday afternoon in August, the day before my grandmother's birthday. I whipped up a three-tiered almond cake covered with butter-cream frosting. My younger sister and I loaded gifts and the cake into my first car. I was only fifteen, my sister was fourteen, neither of us legal to drive by ourselves, but out in the Ozarks, it didn't matter. It was a thirty-five-mile drive to Grandma's along back-woods gravel roads. Our town's three-man police department didn't much care about two teenagers driving to their grandma's.

We had the windows rolled down, our hair blowing in the wind. "*Yooou're* my . . . brown-eyed girl" we sang along with Van Morrison on the radio. We crossed a concrete-slab bridge over a clear blue creek. Many past summers we had gone there to swim. In fact, we were wearing our swimsuits under our clothes just in case.

My sister took a breath and blew the bangs off her face. "You thinking what I'm thinking?"

"You know it!" I said, pulling the car over into a clearing. There were still a few hours of daylight left. Why waste it? We stripped down to our swimsuits, plunged into the cool water and instantly got in a splash fight. Our laughs echoed through the woods.

Out of the corner of my eye I noticed a shiny white extended-cab pickup pass over the bridge. The driver, a man in a white cowboy hat, turned his head to look at us. A few minutes later another pickup passed over. The driver was so short his head barely peeked over the steering wheel. I noticed shadows creeping across the water. It was getting late. "We'd better get going," I said.

We headed back to the car. I couldn't believe it! We had a flat tire. "Oh man. Must have been a sharp piece of gravel," I said. "We'll have to put on the spare."

My sister had turned white.

"What?" I asked.

"The two on this side are flat too."

All the tires had been slashed.

We huddled in the car, wrapped in some old towels, wondering what to do. It was a twenty-mile walk home. Fifteen to Grandma's. I had told Mom we'd probably stay the night there. What if she didn't call to check on us?

"We'll just change back into our clothes, sleep in the car and walk out in the morning," I said to my sister. "It'll be like a campout." I tried to sound confident, as if the slashed tires had just been a nasty prank. Nothing to worry about.

Darkness came quickly, as it always does in the hills. We fell asleep. Later I woke, needing to go to the bathroom. The woods were bathed in moonlight. I stepped out of the car, barefoot, into the forest. The croaks and chirps of the tree frogs and cicadas seemed louder than usual. I checked my watch. Eleven o'clock. Our parents must have thought we were safe at Grandma's.

Suddenly I saw the gleam of a white truck parked across the bridge. Why was it…

Strong arms grabbed me from behind. "Well, what do we got here?" a voice growled. I caught a whiff of whiskey. The man in the white cowboy hat.

"Let go of me!" I screamed, wrestling to escape his grip.

"No," he said, squeezing me tighter. "Not until I'm done with you."

He was at least six feet six and about three hundred pounds. No way I could fight back.

My sister ran from the car and beat at his back. He swatted her to the ground. The short man emerged from the trees. He snatched my sister up and dragged her away. *No!* I reached up, grabbed the cowboy's hat and flung it into the water.

"That's my new hat, you little…" He dropped me and stumbled to the creek.

My sister struggled with the short man. I ran to her. But the cowboy came up behind me. He dragged me to his truck like a rag doll, threw me down in the backseat. He tore at my blouse. I pushed and kicked, screaming even though there was no one else around for miles.

"You know, I'm a professional bull rider," he said with a laugh. He ran his hand up the bare skin of my thigh. I punched his chest. No effect. The other truck roared off. Where was it taking my sister? I sobbed uncontrollably.

All at once, I heard a tremendous crash. Crunching metal and shattering glass. The man pulled off me and jumped out of the truck. His buddy had slammed into a tree across the creek. I climbed out and saw my sister running toward me over the bridge. I grabbed hold of her arm and jerked her into the forest. Roots and rocks ripped at our bare feet as we ran. Flashlight beams tracked us. I heard the men shouting, cursing, getting closer. I pulled my sister to the ground and whispered in her ear, "Don't move. Don't make a sound." I sucked in a silent breath, praying, *Dear God, save us. You are our only hope. Make us invisible.*

I clasped my sister's hand and closed my eyes. I heard their heavy footsteps, and the sticks they carried, sweeping the leaves and underbrush. Closer and closer. I dared to open my eyes. The man in the cowboy hat towered over me, breathing heavily. The smell of liquor. The glare of his flashlight. All he had to do was look down. I squeezed my sister's hand tighter. *Invisible,* I prayed.

The man looked down. Right at us. Stared. Then looked away. The short man staggered up to him, his boots inches from my sister's head. "Come on, let's get out of here," he said, slurring his words.

"No, we'll find them." The cowboy's voice was as cold as ice. His eyes darted all around, left, right, up, down. "They couldn't have just disappeared."

I don't know how long we lay there. We stayed like that, nestled like deer on the forest floor until light began to fill the sky. Only then did we get up. Stiff and cold we crept toward our car. No sign of the men or their trucks. We put on our shoes and prepared for the long walk home.

Just then we heard a truck coming up the gravel road. My heart raced. We almost ran back into the trees. But the old farm truck was familiar. "Dad!" I shouted.

He gathered us in his arms, in a fierce hug, as if he didn't know whether to kiss us or kill us. "We called down to Grandma's house this morning and were scared out of our wits to find you weren't there," he said. "What on earth happened here?"

It was a good question. One I've thought about for thirty-nine years.

SWEPT AWAY
by Susan Harsin

I stepped out onto the cornfield, my tennis shoes sinking into the waterlogged ground. I tried to block out the overpowering smell of fish. But I couldn't block out the scene of destruction that greeted my husband, Darren, and me.

How could this happen? I wondered. In the distance, I saw a row of cabins, half-submerged in the receding floodwaters of the Missouri River, but I couldn't make out our own—whatever was left of it.

Darren and I had bought the cabin just two years earlier as a weekend retreat. It was in an idyllic spot, right on the river, where we could escape with our sons to fish and swim and have cookouts. Darren and the boys had spent weekend after weekend fixing it up, and by the time they were finished, the thirty-year-old structure had doubled in size, with an added dining area, family room, and kitchen.

It was completed just in time for Easter. We invited twenty-five family members over to celebrate. We held an Easter service by the river and cooked up a big feast. I daydreamed about the good times we would have there one day with our grandkids.

Just five weeks later, record-breaking snow melts in Montana combined with heavy spring rains were producing more water than the great Missouri River could handle. The dams and reservoirs upriver overflowed, and the Army Corps of Engineers had no choice but to open the floodgates, unleashing a torrent of water downstream.

We appeared to be the only vacation-cabin owners to return that day. The receding river was still above flood stage and full of debris. Armed with a camera, we were planning to document the damage for our insurance company. I held out hope that some things in the cabin could be salvaged, before mold set in and ruined everything.

The road had been washed out by the flood, so our plan was to trek across the cornfield and swim the rest of the way if necessary. We were both good swimmers. If we got a little wet, so be it.

Now, as we crossed the field, the water crept up from our ankles to our knees. I kept my eyes on the horizon, looking for the cabin. I shivered and rubbed my arms. It was colder than I'd thought. The water was deeper too. I wished I'd worn something more than a tank top and shorts.

"There it is!" I shouted. I could see the back of our cabin, about two hundred yards away. The water was up to its windowsills, the siding was hanging off and it had been gouged in places by debris carried along in the flood. Suddenly the ground beneath us began to slip away. The water was up to my hips now. I jerked the camera from around my neck and held it above my head.

"I don't know if we should still do this," Darren said. "Maybe we should turn back."

"We're almost there," I said. I took another step. My foot flailed for solid ground. I finally touched bottom with my toes, but I couldn't keep my footing. I was being tugged by a current. I grabbed Darren's arm.

"Okay, let's turn back," I gasped.

Too late. The submerged cornfield had become a part of the Missouri itself. I dug my toes into the bottom, but the icy, murky water was too strong, dragging me away from dry land, toward the deep channel of the river. Darren too. He snatched the camera from me.

"Forget about this!" he shouted. "We have to swim for it."

I fought, kicking and wheeling my arms, struggling to hold my head above the surface. I choked and gasped for air. Tree limbs, flowerpots, and yard ornaments rushed furiously by, but there was nothing to hold on to. I kicked harder and sent a desperate plea to God. *Please, Lord, rescue us. Send help.*

We were swept right past our cabin. Up ahead, a tangled mess of debris was trapped in a grove of trees—splintered patio chairs, mangled barbed-wire fencing, a rusted backyard grill, shattered remains of picnic tables, aluminum siding, windows ripped from their frames. And we were rushing headlong toward it.

"No!" I screamed. I tried to swim away from the dangerous-looking pile. My heart raced. I was no match for the river. "Look out!" Darren yelled.

We both slammed up against a large box wedged in the wreckage. We hit it so hard that the lid popped open, followed by an incredible, brilliant burst of color.

"Darren, look!"

Inside the box right in front of us—two foam pool noodles! One neon orange and one hot pink.

We grabbed the floating noodles and wrapped them around our waists. Immediately, their buoyancy lifted us.

We pushed away from the debris and floated down the channel. Now we could navigate to where the floodwaters had receded. Finally, we pulled ourselves out and collapsed in the mud, gulping deep, thankful breaths of air.

"How on earth…," Darren said, unwrapping the pool toy from his waist and gently squeezing the foam, as if making sure it was real.

Someone, somewhere along the Missouri, had a pool and a pool box, most likely. Swept along in the wave of that historic flood, two helpless humans had been directed toward it. Us.

We sloshed back to our car, shivering and wet. We still have the noodles, to remind us that when everything seems lost, help is within arm's reach.

A PRAYER FOR FLIGHT 232

by Renee Knudsen

My younger siblings and I were in the backseat of the family minivan. I was holding a steaming cardboard box of pizza on my lap. The clock on the dashboard read 5:17 PM, and we were starving. "Let's get home while it's still hot," we begged. The car smelled of cheese and pepperoni, and every second we delayed was torture.

Mom started to turn the key in the ignition—and then stopped. "Kids," she said, suddenly, urgently, "we need to pray." I heard the concern in her voice. "Let's pray. Right now. For Dad."

Normally we didn't pray like this, but my brothers, sisters, and I all bowed our heads and prayed for Dad's safety. I wasn't so hungry anymore. Was Dad okay?

That same evening, six hundred miles away at LaGuardia Airport in New York City, my father was sitting in the cockpit of a commercial airliner, preparing for takeoff. The copilot looked over the instrument panel. "Check. That's everything, Captain," he told Dad.

As my father crossed the last item off of his preflight checklist, the flight attendant popped her head into the cockpit. "Everyone's seated, Captain. We've got a full plane today: one hundred and thirty-nine people."

Dad taxied toward the runway. Once in position, Dad stopped the plane and waited for clearance from air-traffic control. Pretty soon a voice came crackling over the radio: "Flight 232, you are now clear for takeoff."

But instead of barreling down the runway at 150 miles per hour, Dad hesitated.

The copilot stared at him. "Captain?" he said.

"We're not accepting that clearance for takeoff," Dad told him.

"What? Why?" the copilot asked.

"We're not accepting that clearance," Dad repeated, standing firm.

Later that evening, Mom got a call from Dad. We all gathered around her as they spoke on the phone, eager to learn if anything had occurred. "See you soon, honey," she told Dad finally, and hung up.

With a trace of tears in her eyes, Mom turned to us kids.

"Mom, is everything okay?" my older brother asked.

"Is Dad all right?" I piped up.

Mom told us the story. "This afternoon your father was sitting on the runway when he got the clearance for takeoff. LaGuardia Airport is always busy, so when you get a clearance, you go. But for some reason he sensed that he should wait. Sensed it very clearly."

"What happened?" my sister asked.

My mother put her arm around my youngest brother. "Seconds later he and his copilot heard a rumble. Just then, a 747 broke out of the clouds and landed—on the very same runway that had just been cleared for Dad. If he hadn't waited those extra seconds, the two planes would have collided."

We all sat in wonder. Had our prayers really saved our father from an unthinkable disaster? There was only one way to be sure. "What time was this?" I asked.

My mother wiped her eyes. "5:17 PM," she said.

CHAPTER 4

You Will Be Healed

SHIELDED
by Dave Hess

I thanked God that morning for the water-stained ceiling tiles. They were as much a miracle to me as a clear blue sky. When I opened my eyes after a fitful night's sleep and saw them above my hospital bed, I knew I was still alive. I was pretty sure there were no ceiling tiles in heaven.

I was thirty-nine years old, and wasn't likely to live out the week, much less see forty. As the morning dragged on, my family and the parishioners of my church came in and out of my room, praying for my recovery. Prayer was all I had left. It was Franny, one of my older congregants, who seemed to have the most faith in the impossible. "Pastor Dave, I'm not sure what this means, but you will find the Lord to be a shield around you. . . . That's in the Bible somewhere, or maybe a hymn. I just know He wanted me to tell you that."

I recognized the phrase, from one of David's psalms: "You are a shield around me, O Lord." But those kinds of miracles, the big biblical ones? They just didn't apply today.

I'd come through the worst of my battle with acute myeloid leukemia, just completed my final round of chemo. Through it all, my wife, Sheri, stood by me, wearing a hospital gown and a mask to protect my compromised immune system. It looked like I was going to be okay. The oncologist was pleased with my latest test results. I'd even been able to dance, briefly, with our daughter in my hospital room just before she'd left for the prom. Then something happened that made it all for naught—my appendix burst.

Sheri was at our son's soccer game when she got the call. My white blood cells were depleted from the chemo—I couldn't fight infection. My platelet count was low—my blood wouldn't clot. In other words, surgery was not an option. And without it, the poison flooding my body would be fatal.

The doctors inserted a tube into my abdomen, hoping to drain off some of the toxins. But it would only buy me hours, not the weeks I needed to build up the strength to survive an appendectomy. Sheri raced to the hospital and told everyone we knew to come, come now.

A procession of visitors murmured their prayers, said good-bye. Except Franny. She was so sure of the message she'd received. I didn't have the heart to tell her otherwise.

The nurses doped me up to keep me comfortable. I lost track of time. Soon, the sun had set again. My visitors left. Sheri went home to look after the kids.

Holy Spirit is a Catholic hospital, and Scripture readings are broadcast over the PA system at the beginning and end of each day. I could no longer hear those words of hope. In seminary, I learned that fear is not an emotion—it's a spirit. And this evil spirit spoke louder. I pictured Sheri sitting alone at home, mustering all her courage to hold the family together. I saw my daughter in her wedding gown, walking down the aisle without me. I saw our sons playing pickup football, no one to cheer them on.

"You are gone, they are alone," the spirit whispered.

I countered it with all I had, Franny's strange message and David's prayer at the forefront of my mind. "You are a shield around me, O Lord," I said out loud. I repeated it over and over until I was able to sleep.

I woke up the next day and saw the ceiling tiles. The day after that too. My doctors and nurses knew of only one case where anyone with cancer like mine survived a burst appendix for so long. When I passed the one-week mark, a social worker said they were sending me home, but that I'd have to come in every few days for blood tests to see if I was strong enough for surgery. There was no guarantee I would be.

I treasured every moment with my family. Sheri read to me in bed. I played piano with the kids, and we sang, talked, and laughed until I couldn't keep my eyes open. I even spent time with our dog, cuddling on the sofa. Laying my hands on my children's heads, I prayed for them as if it were the last time I could. "Lord, let all heaven break loose upon them as they fulfill their destinies."

Each morning, Sheri helped me out of the shower and I stared in the mirror at the tubes hanging out of my chest, the ports from chemotherapy. I looked like the Terminator on a bad day. Somehow, though, I made it six weeks. My platelet levels normalized. The surgeon prepared me for the operation. "I'm going to do an exploratory procedure," he said. "We need to see what damage has been done."

Through the fog of anesthesia, I remembered David's words. Why those? Franny wasn't sure what they meant, and neither was I. But that passage had sustained me, like provisions during a desolate winter. *You are a shield around me.*

I opened my eyes to the hospital ceiling tiles, Sheri squeezing my hand. The surgeon came in, holding some five-by-seven-inch glossy photos taken from inside my lower abdomen. "Have you ever had an operation before?" he asked.

"Only my tonsils," I said.

"I've never seen anything like this," the surgeon said. He held up one of the photos. It just looked like blobs to me. "Here is your appendix, what's left of it," he said, pointing with his pen. "But surrounding it...is a kind of tent, composed of adhesions." He made a circle. "It's the strongest kind of scar tissue there is. We normally see it only after someone has surgery."

"What does that mean?" I asked.

The surgeon fumbled for the right words. "All the toxins were contained within this structure. These adhesions, they acted almost like... tiny shields, tightly packed together."

I'll never know why my life was spared, not while I'm here on earth. That's what heaven is for. For now, I enjoy my family, my friends, the blue sky. I'm not ready to see beyond the ceiling tiles quite yet.

OUT OF THIN AIR
by Patti Curtin

My chest tightened. It felt like a clamp was shutting off air from my lungs. I dug in my purse for my rescue inhaler. Oh no, I'd left it in our car, 1,200 feet down the mountain. My husband, Tom, rubbed my back, worried. My wheezing worsened as we waited for the chairlift down. *What if I don't make it?*

A calm voice whispered in my ear, "Just pray."

All afternoon, we'd hiked Bristol Mountain in New York's Finger Lakes region, taking in panoramic views of the fall foliage. I'd paused for one last photo, then run to catch up with Tom at the summit. That's when I began wheezing. Now I was having a full-blown asthma attack. Panic would only make it worse, so I took Tom's whispered advice. I closed my eyes and prayed. *Dear God, I surrender my fear to You and trust that You will rescue me.*

The air around me suddenly shifted. Tom's hand held mine, but on my other side, I sensed another presence standing close. Warmth welled up in my chest and radiated through my airways. Someone was breathing into me, like a lifeguard performing CPR, opening my lungs. Was this a dream? Was I dying? I opened my eyes. I was still standing, Tom by my side. Just Tom. He helped me onto the next chairlift. I inhaled deeply as we descended through the crisp air. Finally, our feet touched ground and we stepped off.

"I'll run to the car. You stay here," Tom said.

"No, I'm all right," I said. I tried to describe the presence, the warmth of borrowed breath. "Thanks for reminding me to pray."

"Pray?" Tom looked puzzled. "I didn't tell you to pray. I was too scared to say a word."

HEALED

by Sam Vaught

I was never going to get better. In fact, I was going to get worse. A vein attached to my retina had hemorrhaged. An occlusion, the doctor called it. The pressure from the blood slowly building up behind my right eye was nearly unbearable. Laser surgery would relieve the pain but not stem the loss of vision in my eye. In time, macular degeneration would cause my left eye to go blind as well. It was already starting. Darkness was taking over. Just when I thought a new life was beginning.

My wife, Shirley, and I had retired and were finishing up our dream house. I'd started my own bluegrass group, Uncle Sam & the Gospel Gang. These were supposed to be my golden years. Golden? Black was more like it. Blind. And the darkness ran deeper than my eyesight. It blotted my soul. I'd always been a faithful man, but if there was hope for me, I couldn't see it. All I heard was, "There's nothing more to be done, Mr. Vaught."

It was April, time for the town's annual ramp festival, celebrating the wild onions that grow abundantly around these parts in the spring. Fry 'em up with potatoes and cheese and you've got yourself a delicious dish. People come from miles around for the feast. My wife and I joined the group cleaning the ramps, peeling away the outer layer, washing off the dirt and cutting off the ends. It was hard work, but fun with friends.

"I'm not going," I had told Shirley earlier. "I'd be lucky not to cut my fingers off."

"Sam, you can do this," she said. "It'll be good to get out of the house."

I'd relented. Now I sat at the table by a mound of onions and started in. I held each stalk firmly against the table, carefully slicing through the end. Glancing to my left, I saw the pile Shirley had already gone through, while I'd cleaned less than a dozen. I focused what was left of the sight in my one good eye back on my work.

"You know what you get when you mix onions with baked beans?" I heard a woman across the table say. "Tear gas." Everyone laughed, even me. I looked over at her, a woman about my age. A man I took to be her husband sat beside her. I'd never seen them before. Must have been their first time. The look on her face was pure joy. Like this was the best day of her life. I marveled at how she sliced the ends off her ramps without even looking at them. *If only*, I thought.

There was something infectious about her. She kept the room in stitches. The day flew by. I looked at the heaping pile of roots I'd cut. I'd done better than I thought.

"It's been a pleasure," the woman said, standing up. "I just thank God for all His blessings. He hasn't failed me yet." She reached back a bit awkwardly and felt around for a long white cane leaning against the wall, then made her way out of the building, her husband gently holding her arm.

She's blind? She'd handled those ramps like a pro. Handled herself with such grace. Blessed—that's how she'd described herself. I felt a faint echo of hope reverberate through me.

I underwent the surgery to relieve the pressure on my eye. Like the doc said, the pain was gone, but my vision was no better. Still, something was different. I couldn't help thinking about how that woman *accepted* her blindness joyously, almost gratefully.

I started singing at churches and nursing homes. Heck, I could always play and sing with my eyes closed anyway. Evenings I'd sit on the deck with my wife, listening to the birds and breathing in the night air. I savored the sounds, the warmth of a touch, the sweetness of smell, a world as rich and full and beautiful as any I could see.

One evening at church, the preacher asked if anyone needed anointing. Not sure why, I raised my hand. The congregation surrounded me and placed their hands on me while the minister prayed. In each individual hand, I could feel love. An unmistakable feeling of comfort. The same feeling I'd had for months. Truth was, I'd already been healed, that day cleaning ramps. I was healed of the darkness that blotted my soul.

Two weeks later, Shirley and I were driving down the highway. Suddenly, the road, the cars, the trees on either side of us—all were crystal clear. I closed my left eye. The world was still there. "Shirley, I can see!" I shouted. "I can see everything!"

My doctor could hardly believe it, let alone explain it. But there I was in her office reading the eye chart like nothing had ever happened.

HOLDING ON

by Gayle Brisbane

I ran down the hospital corridor, the doctor's words echoing in my mind—"You'd better come quick. We're losing her."

My husband, Bert, and I burst through the doors of the Neonatal Intensive Care Unit and stopped short. All those weeks of hoping, praying, I imagined the day that we'd bring our newborn girls home with us—all three of them. Never this. Two of my babies clung to life, and the third was slipping away. The doctors stood around little Abby's incubator, their faces drawn. The nurses who'd tended to her for weeks choked back tears. I had no reason left to hope. *This is good-bye.*

Not so long before, I'd given up on starting a family. I'd gotten married when I was twenty, but it ended in divorce by the time I was twenty-six. I watched my older brothers get married and have kids, while I struggled to meet someone new. I was a sports reporter for the local TV station; there had to be some guy who would be interested in me. But nothing worked out. Countless times I cried out to God, depressed and tired of feeling so alone. When I turned forty, I thought that was it.

Until Bert came along. We met at the gym. He was ambitious, with a good job in finance. For a big, strong man, he was a softy on the inside. I fell for him in no time. He was my answer to prayer. He proposed to me at home in Phoenix—he hid the ring in my purse—and we were married nine months later. We both wanted to have children, even though we knew that at my age, it would be problematic. The doctor told us I only had a two percent chance of getting pregnant naturally, so I underwent in vitro fertilization. Surprisingly, it worked the first time around.

Then came the sonogram. I was pregnant with identical triplet girls! I pictured us walking on the beach, the five of us hand in hand. The girls dressed in matching white sundresses with bows in their hair, kicking at the sand. It was as if God was helping me make up for lost time.

Less than five months into my pregnancy, I collapsed at work. There was a lot of bleeding. My whole body shook with fear. I was rushed to the hospital. Test after test brought more bad news. The placenta had separated from my uterine wall. I developed gestational diabetes. The triplets contracted fetofetal transfusion syndrome—they were fighting each other for nutrients. I prayed that I'd make it to seven months so the girls would have a better chance at life. But by six months, they were ready to come out. Two days after Valentine's Day, Abby, Bella, and Simone were born. They weighed less than four and a half pounds—combined.

Abby and Bella underwent surgery for perforated intestines, followed by heart surgery. Simone's lungs were collapsing. Abby needed three blood transfusions. Each procedure produced new complications. Bert and I practically lived at the hospital, praying nonstop by their incubators and watching helplessly while the nurses administered rounds of painkillers, steroids, and antibiotics. At one month old, Bella and Simone were critical but stable. It was Abby we were losing. She'd contracted an *E. coli* blood infection that sent her body into septic shock.

Now I had to ask a question, though I didn't think I could endure hearing the answer. The doctor on call was a visiting neonatologist—he practiced at the hospital only one week out of the month, but he'd been following my girls' case closely.

"Isn't there anything else we can do?" I said.

"Medically speaking, no," he said. "We've done everything."

"So that's it?"

He hesitated. "I called you down here to try one last thing—kangaroo care."

I'd spent enough time around the NICU to know a little about kangaroo care—a way for moms and dads to bond with their newborn. The baby, dressed in just a diaper, was placed on the parent's bare chest, skin to skin. Some mothers I'd met at the hospital swore it helped improve breathing and sleep patterns. Abby's concerns were far graver. She was barely holding on. Kangaroo care? That was it? Abby was about to take her last breaths; wasn't there medicine, another surgery, a piece of machinery, anything that could help?

"We don't fully understand kangaroo care," the doctor admitted. "With all our technology, it seems old-fashioned. But there's something real that happens, something mysterious, just from contact. We've seen it improve the survival rate of premature newborns."

I looked down at Abby. What we needed was a miracle. The slightest intake of breath was a struggle for her. Her entire right arm was an open wound, burned by the sodium bicarbonate she'd been given to balance her toxic blood levels. She still weighed less than two pounds, but had ballooned to twice her size from all the fluids pumped into her fragile little body. It hurt to look at her. She was dying before my eyes.

"Gayle, we have to try something," Bert said. "Even this." I knew he was right. Maybe kangaroo care wouldn't heal her. It seemed so basic after all the doctors had done, all that technology and knowledge. But it was a chance to say good-bye. I'd hold her close so she'd know I loved her. One last time.

The nurse placed Abby in my arms and wrapped a blanket around us. I was afraid I might hurt her. I held her gently against the warmth of my skin, singing "You Are My Sunshine," not sure if she could hear me. *It's okay, Abby. You don't have to hold on any longer.*

My tears dripped onto Abby's head. I thought of my perfect family image on the beach. The picture had changed. Now there were two girls instead of three. *No!* I thought. *I don't want to let you go.* I didn't want to change the picture.

I pressed Abby closer to my chest. *Don't go! You are so loved. Your sisters need you. Dad needs you. I need you. Don't go, my sweet girl.* I felt my words go through me to her. Could she hear me? She didn't move, but I could sense the faintest heartbeat. It seemed to be growing stronger. I held her for an hour, feeling the tiny thump-thump against my chest. Next it was Bert's turn. He closed his eyes, cradling her close. She looked so small against his bare chest. "Stay with us, Abby," he whispered.

The nurse put Abby back into her incubator. We huddled around and watched her vitals. *Come on, Abby.* Her blood pressure started to rise. I squeezed Bert's hand. Her oxygen levels were stabilizing. Her heart rate was too. *You can do it, Abby!*

Abby was still weak, but she made it through the night.

We continued doing kangaroo care with Abby as often as we could. After more than thirteen weeks in the intensive care unit, we brought the girls home—all three of them. The doctors couldn't explain Abby's recovery.

"Perhaps the child needs to know someone out there loves them," one of the neonatologists suggested. "You do all you can medically. Sometimes, though, it takes a different power."

Love is that power. I have no doubt whatsoever that love brought Abby back from the very brink of death when all else failed and all hope was gone. It was love that gave my daughter life.

ILLUMINATING SYMPTOMS
by Freida Thornton

The diagnosis. The mastectomy. Reconstructive surgery. Everything about my breast cancer had been rough, but by far the worst part was the fear. Even on good days it never quite went away. Sometimes all the stress made me light-headed. It was getting to my husband, Alton, too. Normally he was a pillar of strength and health, but lately he'd been getting bad headaches.

I'd tried to hold on to the hopeful news from my previous checkup. "It looks like the surgeon got everything," Dr. Pittman had said. "The new breast tissue looks healthy." But now, as he reexamined me, my fears returned.

Dr. Pittman studied my skin for longer than usual, frowning. That couldn't be good. He finally looked up. "I can't believe I'm asking this, Freida, but have you been smoking?"

"I've never smoked in my life!" I said.

"Anyone been smoking at home?"

I shook my head.

He looked perplexed. "The reconstructed breast looked fine right after surgery. Now the skin has turned gray, indicating exposure to something like smoke, affecting the blood supply."

The room spun. "Is it the cancer?"

"No, but the discoloration could mean the new tissue is dying. I want to see you again in a few weeks." I went home more fearful than ever.

The next day Alton's brother, Bob, came by. "How are you?" he said.

"Pretty well, I thought, but..." I told him about the skin discoloration and what my doctor had said about smoke.

Bob sniffed the air. "It does smell funny. Not like smoke. Something else."

Neither Alton nor I had noticed anything. Still, I called our heating company. They sent a repairman at once.

"Good thing you called," the repairman said. "You've got a natural gas leak that's giving off carbon monoxide. A slow one like this might only cause headaches and dizziness, but if it got any worse..." He didn't need to say more.

I didn't think I could feel more grateful. Till my next checkup, that is, when the doctor examined me again—and couldn't find anything to be concerned about. "The new tissue is completely healthy," Dr. Pittman said. "It's like that discoloration was never there."

WIDE AWAKE
by Robert E. Lohstroh Jr.

There is a photo on the wall in my house. A framed picture of a beautiful young woman with honey-blonde hair falling past her shoulders and a sweet, shy smile. She's not my wife, my sister, or my daughter. Not even a friend. I never knew her while she was alive. But she means everything to me.

Here's the sad fact of the matter: She lost her life at age twenty-eight and I regained mine at age fifty-six. Even staring at those two numbers I struggle to find God's justice in them, to see where His mercy lies. But it would be wrong of me to question His plan. Instead, I express gratitude for every day I have left, for every breath given to me.

A half dozen years ago I was diagnosed with a deadly combination of emphysema and chronic bronchitis. My lungs were severely damaged, and I was placed on oxygen 24–7. Finally, the doctor said those words no patient ever wants to hear: "There is nothing more we can do for you." Nothing more than a double lung transplant. If I should survive long enough to get one.

When you become a candidate for a transplant—and I was considered a good risk because apart from my lungs I was healthy—you are put on a list. It's a bit like living on death row, waiting for a reprieve. Every day, you wonder if you will be called. Every day that you aren't feels like another death sentence. Although you try not to think about it, it's a matter of odds. Where are you on the list? Are you close to the top? Who will die so that you can live?

I tried not to think about that, but to simply trust in God. Trust in His plan. But that got a lot harder when I was moved from the list at the Cleveland Clinic to Methodist Hospital in Indianapolis. The former does more than five times the number of lung transplants than the latter each year.

By June I was struggling to breathe even on eight liters of oxygen per day. The slightest task drained me. I knew that I wouldn't live to see my birthday in August.

Then I got the call. July 20. They thought they had a set of lungs that would match my body size, blood, and tissue type. Was this the reprieve I'd hoped and prayed for? I was rushed to the hospital. They ran me through a barrage of tests and wheeled me into surgery.

Within twenty-four hours of the call, I was in the ICU, recovering. Awake. Lucid. I took a breath. And another. Cool air rushed into my chest. I kept drawing it in, filling my new lungs to capacity before exhaling. Never had something so basic to life seemed like such a divine gift. Never had a breath tasted sweeter.

I went from the ICU to a private room, gaining strength each day but sleeping fitfully. Someone had died to give me this miracle. That was always on my mind. I didn't want to think about what the donor's family was going through. That thought, more than the beeping monitors and the nurses coming in to check on me, kept me awake and restless.

On my fourth night in the hospital, I found myself staring at the clock, watching the minutes tick by. It was 2:00 AM and the room was lit only by a ribbon of light coming from the open door. I could hear the nurses talking at the nurses' station and then footsteps.

Someone appeared in the doorway, the light like an aura behind her. A young woman in a hospital gown.

She stepped into the room and took two paces toward me.

"Who are you?" I asked. "Are you my nurse just coming on duty?"

"I am your organ donor," she said. "I wanted to check on you and tell you that everything is going to be all right."

I couldn't respond. I just stared at her, this young woman illuminated by the hallway light, taking in every detail of her features. Her face was aglow.

Then she turned and walked back into the hallway, disappearing as quickly as she had come.

Mentally I pinched myself. No, I wasn't dreaming. Yes, I knew what I'd experienced was impossible. My donor could not have appeared at my bedside. It had to be someone else. But who was she and why did her words give me such sudden relief and reassurance?

For very good reasons, you can never get in touch with your donor's family unless they reach out to you. Even then, hospital protocol precludes any contact for months. But I wrote a letter to the donor's family expressing my gratitude and my sympathy, and gave it to a hospital administrator. It was the least I could do.

To my surprise, I soon received a letter in return. It was from the mother of my donor. She asked me to give her a call.

She was warm and kind, all the things I hoped for, and was happy to meet with me. A kind of closure, perhaps for both of us.

Her twenty-eight-year-old daughter, Priscilla, had died in a car accident. The family had been devastated by such a tragic loss. I hoped to show the mother that something good had come from it.

We met for lunch, and I told her about the blessing of her daughter's gift. How my daily death sentence had been lifted. I even told her about the strange visitor to my hospital room. My story seemed to give her some comfort.

"What about your daughter?" I asked. "She must have been really wonderful."

"She was," her mother said and poured out her heart.

When she was done, she reached into her purse and removed a photograph for me to see.

That was when I took my deepest breath yet. For it is the very same photo I keep on my wall today. Long blonde hair, clear blue eyes, the shy sweet smile.

The woman who came to my room that night in the hospital.

IMMEDIATE CARE
by Karen Huber

I hurried down the hospital corridor, pushing a man in a wheelchair toward the trauma unit, praying for his life. Moments before, I'd made a critical decision, perhaps a life-altering one. Had I saved a life? Or would my competence as a triage nurse be called into question?

It had been a hectic morning at the emergency department of Orlando Regional Medical Center. I'm an emergency and trauma nurse with eight years of experience. It was my job to gather information and make judgment calls about the urgency of each patient's complaint. I looked for telltale signs of a severe condition. I couldn't risk a relatively healthy patient taking up a doctor's time while someone else became critically ill in the waiting room. Trust me—I wish no patients had to wait. But that day, by mid-afternoon, our fifty-six beds had been filled and forty more patients remained to be seen.

Then a man came up to the reception desk. "I have pain here," he said simply, pointing to his stomach. His eyes were clear, focused. He was breathing normally and spoke coherently. *Middle-aged man,* I thought quickly. *Walked in unassisted. Mild abdominal complaint. Could be anything from appendicitis to pancreatitis to gas.* I prepared to do a more in-depth assessment. *Minor? Delayed? Immediate?* I hadn't decided yet.

Just as I was beginning his registration process, a peculiar feeling came over me. I heard the chatter of the patients, the opening and closing of the automatic doors, yet a bubble had enveloped the man and me. Time froze within that bubble. Unmistakably, I heard a distant, calm, yet commanding voice: *This man could die in front of you at any moment.*

I looked around—I was sure I was the only one who had heard the voice. The man looked at me quizzically. I had the option of sending him immediately to trauma, but only if he was a serious case that couldn't wait. My colleagues would question my competence as a triage nurse if it was a false alarm. But I couldn't shake the feeling. *Not minor—immediate.* He could die in front of me.

I grabbed a wheelchair. "Please call trauma," I told a colleague. "Let them know I'm coming with a patient."

My colleague gave a skeptical glance. "Let them know," I repeated. "Now."

We arrived at trauma and the nurse there also eyed us with suspicion. The man certainly hadn't gotten any sicker—flush with color, breathing normally, no sign of distress. "He needs to be here," I insisted.

I returned to my desk, still not believing what had happened. Twenty minutes passed, then the phone rang. It was the nurse from trauma. "Karen, that patient you brought in…" *Here it comes,* I thought. "How did you know?" the nurse said.

"Know what?" I asked.

The man had an aortic dissection, the nurse told me—the major blood vessel leading from his heart had torn. Victims usually displayed no outward signs of danger—until it was too late. I couldn't tell her the whole truth. She wouldn't believe it. "I just got this feeling…," I said.

"It's a good thing you did," the nurse said. "This man could have died in front of you at any moment."

MIRACLE BABY

by Paula Lenneman

A football spirals deep down the field. A strong young man running like the wind reaches out his hands just in time to grab the pass for a completion, maybe even a touchdown.

That was the dream I had for the baby boy I was soon to have, my prayers for a healthy son. Now, though, everything was in doubt.

My eyes froze on the ghostly sonogram of my baby on the monitor, a pulsing inside his tiny body. His heartbeat was strong, the body fully formed, complete and perfect. Except for one small hole where a hole shouldn't be.

"This is where the stomach is pushing up inside the diaphragm, every time the child breathes," the doctor said. "It shouldn't be doing that."

I squeezed my husband, Russ's, hand. This was supposed to be a routine test. I could definitely see what the doctor was talking about. It was *all* I could see.

"We'll induce labor in the morning," the doctor said. "The baby will need surgery—immediately. But I'm afraid your child will never have the strength or energy of other children. There will always be a weakness in that spot near his heart and lungs."

"It's going to be okay," Russ said on the drive home. But in his eyes I could see he was as scared as I was.

We spent the evening calling family and friends, begging for prayers. "We'll put you on the prayer chain at church," people said.

It was like sending out a spiritual SOS. Finally, there was nothing to do but go to bed. Russ and I prayed together, hoping something had been amiss with the test or equipment. Something. *Lord, please make my baby all right.*

But there wasn't. Another ultrasound in the morning definitively confirmed the problem. "I'm sorry," the doctor said. "There is no doubt. We have to get this baby delivered and into surgery."

Only the baby wouldn't cooperate. My contractions grew more frequent, and painful. The wait was excruciating. I thought of all the people praying for us. *Pray harder please,* I thought. *I want my baby to be all right.*

The morning dragged on, past midday, then into evening. Russ stayed at my side. "Just relax," he said. "There are so many people praying for you. Just let it happen." I knew that. Why was God taking so long? All I could think about was the hole inside my son's chest.

Just after midnight, my son's head emerged. He was out. I'd scarcely heard his cries before the doctor cradled my son in his arms and rushed him away.

What if they can't fix the hole? I wondered. *What if something goes wrong? I never even got to hold him.*

"Try to get some sleep," someone said. "We'll let you know as soon as we hear from the surgeon."

I was groggy. Maybe it was just a few hours, maybe one. I lost track.

When we met with the doctor, he appeared in shock. "We didn't do the surgery," he said, his voice quiet.

My heart pounded. "Is our baby okay?" I asked. "What's wrong?"

"He's doing fine," the doctor said. "Just before the operation the surgeon asked for an X-ray. And, well, I can't explain this, but the hole is gone. It's just not there anymore. Someone will be here to take you to him soon. Congratulations." Then he was off.

I could scarcely believe what I was hearing. The hole *was* there. I saw it myself. So did Russ. I stared at him. Was this a mistake? It didn't make any sense.

Tears of relief, tears of joy, rolled down my cheeks. A nurse came in the room and asked if everything was okay.

"I'm just so happy about my baby," I said. "He was supposed to have surgery...."

"You're the mother of the miracle baby!" the nurse exclaimed. "We just had a staff meeting about you. The doctor showed us all the ultrasound images of your son. He asked us what we thought. We all said the same thing. 'The baby needs surgery.' Then he showed us the X-ray. We didn't believe him when he said no surgery had been performed. Everyone was just in awe."

Miracle baby. That's what everyone said. Friends from all over called when we got home. Prayers had gone out across the country. A network of praying people answering our spiritual SOS, from California to Florida.

While I was in labor those fifteen hours, something happened. Something no one, not even the doctors, could explain.

And today, when I watch Michael take the field as wide receiver for his college football team, I remind myself that I am watching a miracle.

A HOPELESS CASE

by Irma DeWaters

I'd never seen a doctor pray before. His palms clasped gently around the thin, weak hand of his patient. His eyes shut tight, a single tear gliding down his cheek. His voice soft, yet strong enough to make the din of the busy hospital fade into the background.

"Lord, she is so young. Please, Father, help me find the way to help her."

It was the last thing I wanted to hear. Not when that patient was me.

February 1974. The steady beat of a heart monitor echoed through the thin, translucent plastic of the oxygen tent. Trapped inside, unable to speak, I fought to stay awake. If I closed my eyes, I might never open them again.

Cold, moist, chemical-scented air sent shivers through my body as I recalled the group of nursing students that had visited earlier that day. "We've tried everything for this patient," their instructor said, his voice hushed. "I'm afraid we can't do anything more for her. She's terminal."

Terminal? There must be some mistake, I wanted to scream. How could this instructor tell strangers something that Dr. Smith—a world-renowned pulmonary specialist—never told me? For seven weeks, he and his staff at the hospital here in Everett, Washington, had run a battery of tests and attempted treatments. They still weren't able to make a diagnosis. They had no explanation for how I'd suddenly gone from a healthy twenty-nine-year-old mother of three to a shrunken, pallid creature, struggling to breathe.

Dr. Smith came in sometime after the students left. He shut the door behind him, pulling a chair to my bedside. *He'll have an answer, he must,*

I thought. The oxygen tent crinkled as he unzipped a flap and pulled it back, sandwiching my hand in his.

Prayer? This was his answer? I'd come here hoping that a pulmonologist at the top of his field would be able to cure me.

For the first time in my life I was angry with God. *How can you take me from my children?* I yelled in my mind. *I'm all they have! They have done nothing to deserve this!*

The symptoms had started suddenly. Shortness of breath. Stabbing chest pains when I inhaled. Severe fatigue. Weight loss. Dehydration. First, I was diagnosed with pleurisy—an inflammation of the lining of the lungs—and prescribed antibiotics. But my condition only got worse. One morning I woke up, looked in the mirror and hardly recognized the woman staring back at me. Pale face, sunken cheeks, deep, dark circles under my eyes. My fever spiked to 104.

"We think you're in the third, possibly fourth stage of tuberculosis," my physician explained later that day. "We're admitting you to the hospital immediately. You'll be seen by Dr. Smith. He's one of the top specialists in the country and the best qualified to treat you." I called a neighbor to look after my children. At the hospital I was quarantined on the ninth floor and zipped in the oxygen tent, this plastic prison. There, Dr. Smith did a lung biopsy and blood work.

"You don't have tuberculosis," he said, with the confidence I expected from someone of his stature. "The bad news is that we're not quite sure what you have. We've never seen anything like it. But rest assured, we'll find the cause."

Nothing they tried made any difference. The oxygen tent kept me alive, but it pulled me further away from the world. Through the hazy plastic, visiting family and friends seemed to be standing in another dimension. Their voices were muffled, hard to hear over the machines.

In the beginning, I was allowed to call my children briefly every day, but my voice grew weaker, and eventually, my lack of energy and the pain in my lungs made forming sounds impossible. When the lights went out at night, the sides of the oxygen tent seemed to close in on me. My heart raced and my lungs gasped for air that they were unable to hold.

I closed my eyes and remembered psalms that had always comforted me before, but every day it was harder to believe I'd ever go home. I was disappearing in the oxygen tent, one feeble breath at a time.

Now Dr. Smith was the one praying. "Help me help her. Give me the wisdom to see what's wrong...." A tear fell. Who expected this? The prayer, and the passion behind it, coming from a medical man. From his lips, it didn't sound like desperation. It sounded like belief. Faith that the answer would come to him somehow. If he had that, then shouldn't I?

Please, Lord, I prayed with him, silently, *heal me. Don't leave my children alone.*

The door to the room suddenly breezed open. Dr. Smith released his grip on my hand and wiped his eyes. He quickly zipped the tent back up. Through the plastic, I saw a tall, middle-aged man in a business suit approach. Not a medical student. Not one of the staff I recognized.

I fought to stay awake, hearing muddled bits and pieces of what Dr. Smith and the other man were saying. They were discussing my condition. From what I could gather, the man was a pulmonary specialist in India. Had Dr. Smith called in aid from the other side of the globe? Would a medical expert have actually flown so far to see me?

I felt the cold metal of a stethoscope press against my chest. My eyelids fluttered open again. The Indian doctor leaned over me, listening intently.

Finally he pulled away. "Sarcoidosis," he said. "It's often mistaken for other diseases. I know it by the sound. I've heard it many times in the lungs of patients in India."

Dr. Smith's eyes lit up. "I never even considered that," he said.

"I'm sure of it," the other doctor said. "You must start treatment right away."

Dr. Smith sprang into action. He summoned the nursing staff and issued urgent orders. Immediately, the nurses began injecting new medicine into my IV.

Within days, my lungs opened up. I could take deep breaths. The oxygen tent was removed. I returned to the world again.

Dr. Smith came back to check in on me. "You're doing well," he said. "You'll be back home with your children soon."

"Thank you for calling in that other doctor," I said.

"I didn't," he said, shaking his head. "I'd never seen that man before in my life. But when he introduced himself, I recognized his name. He's a well-known pulmonary specialist in India, and happened to be in Seattle for a conference. He said he was passing by the hospital and stopped in on a whim to see if he could meet me. He said my work inspired him as a doctor."

Dr. Smith looked up. "I wouldn't call it a whim though."

A LITTLE MORE TIME

by Lowell Streiker

I opened the door to the kennel at the veterinary hospital and knelt beside it, my eyes locking with the cloudy ones of my twenty-year-old platinum miniature poodle, Gus. Reaching in, I gently stroked his curly fur, watching his emaciated body quiver with each labored breath.

I'm here for you, I thought. *Just as you were always there for me. You won't be in pain much longer.* The veterinarian stood by, holding the needle, waiting for the word.

That's when I asked God the impossible. *Lord, I can't say good-bye. Not yet. Please spare him,* I prayed. *Just a little while longer. I need him.*

It was already a miracle that Gus had lived as long as he had. He'd been a spry pup when my wife, Connie, and I brought him home, but age had gradually sapped his strength. First it was arthritis, then failing eyesight and hearing loss. Then one evening he threw up his dinner, and seemed disoriented. By the time I got him to the veterinary hospital, he couldn't walk.

For six days and nights, he was kept alive with intravenous drips and catheters. Finally the vet told me he had done all he could do. It was time to let Gus go.

I gazed at Gus and flashed back on a carousel of memories, as if I were watching a home movie.

Gus leaping from the floor into my arms. Standing on his hind legs and licking the pumpkin pies on the kitchen table one Thanksgiving. Tunneling under our backyard fence to visit his canine girlfriend next door. *Not yet!* I thought again. *Just a little while longer.*

Gus began to tremble, as if he were gathering the strength to stand. He set his front legs on the floor and pushed until he was on his feet. He staggered to my side and lifted his head to look at me.

Breaking into tears, I cradled Gus in my arms. The vet pulled back. "Perhaps we can wait one more day," he said. "I haven't seen him this responsive since you brought him in."

I spent the night coming to peace with letting Gus go. But the next day, the vet called with some startling news.

"Gus is walking," he said, sounding amazed. I went to see for myself. Gus's food and water bowls were across the cage, and though he was still weak and unsteady, he made his way to them and took small bites and sips.

"I can't explain such swift improvement in a twenty-year-old dog," the vet said. "It's simply unheard of." He paused. "But if he keeps eating and walking, I see no reason to keep him here."

Gus came home. I filled his food dish, and he scarfed everything down. *He must be eating for both of us,* I thought. Maybe it was the stress of the last week, but I'd barely been able to eat a thing. I shrugged and collapsed on the couch in the living room, weak with what I assumed was relief.

For several months, Gus and I were buddies again. In fact, I could barely match his energy. The old Gus was back! No one could believe it. Connie even had to chastise him for stealing food from the dinner table. Life was good.

Then one day, I couldn't hold dinner down. I felt disoriented.

"I must have picked up a nasty bug," I told Connie.

Gus climbed into my lap and curled up as I called my doctor to make an appointment.

The doctor ran a bunch of tests. What happened next was the word every person dreads hearing.

"Cancer," the doctor said gravely, after all the test results came back. "In both the kidney and the colon." It had probably been growing for several years.

As determined as I was to fight it, the disease fought back. I had two surgeries to remove as much of the tumors as possible, and then began a round of chemotherapy. When I came home from sessions, cuddling with Gus was all that seemed to help the nausea and fatigue. And the ever-deepening depression.

Then the news got worse. My doctor didn't mince words. "Your colon cancer has spread to your lymph nodes," he said. I knew what was coming next. "Statistically, your life expectancy is two years at most."

I went home in a state of profound shock, feeling like a walking corpse. What hope did I have? I might as well stop the excruciating chemo treatments now and just give in. Why put up a fight against the inevitable?

Connie and I hugged each other and cried. Something warm rubbed against my ankle. Gus. He stared at me with those cloudy brown, loving eyes. *I'm not letting you go,* they seemed to say. He nudged me with his nose—his way of saying *Take me for a walk.*

I clipped on his leash and together we set out. The fresh air, the activity, lifted me a bit from my funk. As long as I was alive I still had moments like this. Gus stopped to snuggle against me. *He's here for me, just as I prayed for. As impossible as it was.* Maybe God knew what I hadn't—that I didn't just want to hold on to my friend, I would need him for the challenge ahead. God was telling me not to give up.

It was clear what I had to do. I asked God the impossible, again. *Lord, give me the strength to fight this cancer,* I prayed. *A little while longer.*

That little while longer has been twenty-one years. And as with Gus, the doctors were confounded by my recovery. Gus passed away in his sleep at the age of twenty-four—the longest-living dog our vet had ever seen—but not before helping me every step of the way in my fight against illness, and not before I was declared cancer-free.

CHAPTER 5

The Lord Directs Your Steps

THE IN-LAWS
by Lana Smith

On the eve of my wedding day, one worry nagged me. Steve and I came from different backgrounds. I was a city girl from Scottsdale, Arizona. He was born in Oklahoma and grew up in Kansas. My dad was a trucker, his was a minister. But the boy who bothered me in freshman biology class at McPherson College in Kansas quickly won my heart. He proposed senior year, and we decided to marry at the college church two days after graduation. My parents and Steve's would drive in to celebrate. Living so far from one another, our parents had never met. And my parents weren't that outgoing. Would they get along?

At the rehearsal dinner, I saw Steve's parents looking curiously at my dad. "Don't worry, Lana, they just think he looks familiar," Steve said, trying to put me at ease.

"I hope that's a good thing…," I replied.

The ceremony and reception went beautifully, and afterward we headed to Steve's parents' house for a family dinner. I was anxious to get there, but first we had to stop to wash our car. Steve's friends had mischievously written "Just Married" on it with white shoe polish. "I'm sure our parents are getting on fine without us," Steve told me. But the butterflies in my stomach wouldn't stop.

When we finally pulled up, I was relieved to see our dads happily walking together in the yard. "We figured out how we know each other," Steve's dad said.

Twenty years ago Dad was driving long haul when a snowstorm forced him to detour through Oklahoma. "It was Sunday morning, so I pulled my big rig over and stopped at a church for services," Dad said. "Afterward, the minister and his wife invited me home for a meal."

"That was us!" Steve's dad chimed in.

Later, I told Mom how amazed I was by Dad and Steve's fateful meeting all those years before.

"There's more," Mom said. "Your dad met a lot of people on his routes, but I definitely remember him talking about that couple. He was so impressed by them. He thought it was funny our kids were about the same age...and he told me one more thing."

"What was that?" I asked.

"He said he'd be proud if one of our kids married into a family like theirs."

TRIP OF A LIFETIME
by Eileen Helm Fulton

It was supposed to be a dream vacation for my late husband and me for our thirtieth anniversary, but I was experiencing the joy of Hawaii with my best friend, Sue, that fall. And we'd done everything my husband and I had dreamed of doing—soared above ancient volcanoes in a helicopter; toured Pearl Harbor where so many brave Americans died in December 1941; rented a car and sampled the island cuisine. Tomorrow would be the best—an all-day cruise along the Na Pali Coast.

Yet even in the midst of this tropical dream paradise I felt a lingering sadness, a sense that my life was adrift. In the last three years I'd not only lost my husband but my mom and dad too. And I'd lost some of my faith. Not in God, who'd held me up through each loss and every trial that I had faced—it was a sense that I was losing faith in myself. No dream vacation no matter how fabulous and exotic was going to change that, I feared.

After a day of fun and shopping on Kauai we returned to our hotel room to find the phone button blinking. It was a voicemail from the hotel concierge. "A couple is looking for transportation to the dock for the catamaran cruise along the Na Pali Coast you ladies booked this morning. Would you mind driving them?" We were happy to give them a lift instead of them calling a taxi. Some company might be fun!

The next afternoon we met Janet and Don from Illinois in the lobby. They thanked us profusely for giving them a ride in our rental. The four of us clicked right away, though I couldn't put my finger on just why.

After dinner on the boat that night I walked to the rail to feel the breeze, still trying to shake my sadness, missing my husband. A minute later, Don came to join me. The catamaran rocked and swayed causing us to lock arms, steadying each other. Suddenly, a feeling came over me. It was so incredibly pervasive I had to close my eyes. "Take care of this man. Be there for him," I heard.

Had the Holy Spirit just spoken to me? When I opened my eyes Don was standing in a puddle of water. *Maybe he's going to slip,* I thought, tightening my grip on him and anchoring one foot behind his.

But for the rest of the cruise, Don remained safe while I wondered why I felt such an urge to be protective of this man I barely knew. What was going on?

After the cruise we went back to the hotel and parted ways. "Keep in touch...and take care," I said, looking at Don.

Back home in Michigan the weather turned cool. I dropped an e-mail to Janet and Don saying how nice it was to meet them. I got no response. But I just knew Janet would get back to me.

One night I was watching the news when there was a report about the Good Samaritan living organ donor program that matched potential donors with often desperate recipients. Unfortunately, not enough people volunteered to be donors. All at once I felt an overwhelming desire to find out how I might qualify as a donor for someone. The thought stayed with me for weeks.

Finally I received an e-mail from Janet. "I'm sorry I've taken so long to write," she said. "But when we came home, Don went into kidney failure. That's why we wanted to take our trip, before it was too late. It could be a few years before they find a matching donor, and the list of people who need transplants is long. I'm not qualified as a donor and our two sons are disqualified because of the family history of diabetes. He'll start dialysis soon, much sooner than we thought he'd have to. Hoping for the best. Please keep us in your prayers. Love, Janet."

I was stunned. I stared at Janet's message for a long time, remembering that exact, overwhelming message I'd heard on the catamaran: *Take care of this man. Be there for him.* I e-mailed her back, asking for more information about how I could get tested.

She called me right away. I could sense her shock. "I can't believe someone we met one time would do this for us," she said. "Thank you! Please keep praying." The chances of me being a match were slim, yet I felt called to get tested. I was sure of it.

A transplant coordinator sent me a testing kit. I followed the instructions and sent the lab work. Four days later, the call came.

"Hi, Eileen," the coordinator said. "You're not going to believe this. You're a match! A fantastic match!"

It was almost as if time stopped. Her words hung in the air. I thought about the recent losses in my life. The feeling I was lost. Now I sensed I was on the verge of something inexplicable and miraculous, as if grace was pouring into my life, renewing me, a baptism of hope. As if by giving away a part of myself I would be made whole.

I wanted to tell Don and Janet in a special way. My sister helped me sew a red fabric kidney-shaped tree ornament with embroidered letters that read: "We Match!" I express mailed it to Don just in time for Christmas.

Don called me immediately. "Are you really going to do this?" he said, his voice choked with emotion. Then Janet got on the line. She could hardly speak but to say thank you over and over again, and I tried to explain the feeling I had experienced.

The day of the transplant, Don and I walked to the surgical unit arm in arm, just as we had stood that evening on the catamaran. The operation was a complete success. "It's rare we get such a perfect match," the surgeon said. "Are you sure you're not brother and sister?"

Only in the sense that we all are, all of us living on this earth, connected in ways that we can never dream and filled with grace at the most unexpected moment, any moment that God might choose.

LILLIAN

by Judy Loggia

My ten-year-old, Donna, burst through the front door. "Mom, I made a new friend at school today," she said. "Can she come over tomorrow?" Donna was a shy kid and I had been praying for her to make some friends to bring her out of her shell.

"Sure, honey, that sounds great," I said, thinking back to my own best friend growing up.

Lillian and I lived across the street from each other in Washington Heights, New York. We met at age ten too, and were instantly joined at the hip. Like my daughter, I was introverted, but Lillian drew me out and boosted my confidence. She was one of the friendliest people in school. And beautiful too—with shiny black hair, so shiny it was almost indigo, and a mile-wide smile. I knew we would be best friends forever.

Senior year of high school Lillian went on a trip to Florida, the first time we'd be apart for more than a few days. "I'll be back soon," she told me. But three days later I answered my door to find Lillian's sister standing there, a pall across her face.

"Judy...Lillian's..." She could hardly get the words out. My best friend had drowned on vacation.

Shortly afterward, my family moved to New Jersey. Over the years I lost touch with Lillian's family. But I still thought of her often. Tears formed in my eyes whenever I did. What I wouldn't give to feel close to her again.

The next day Donna brought her new friend home. "Hi, Mrs. Loggia," the little girl said, skipping through the front door. She flipped her hair from her shoulders—hair so shiny and black it was almost indigo—and shot me a giant smile. "My name's Lillian."

That hair. That smile. Lillian. How wonderful—my daughter's new friend was so much like the best friend I had lost.

I was still dizzy from the similarities when Lillian's mom came by to pick her up later that afternoon. I opened the door to let her in.

"Judy!" she screamed. Before I knew it, her arms had wrapped me in a tight hug. Pretty friendly for someone I had never met!

"It's me," she said, laughing. "Lillian's sister, from Washington Heights."

Yes, my daughter's friend looked familiar all right. She was my Lillian's niece. Her namesake.

A RANDOM CUP OF JOE

by Gina Sclafani

Today I sit in Iraq, my family and loved ones in America. But I have new friends and loved ones here who serve with me. I think of the look in that Iraqi soldier's eyes as we helped his sick baby. . . . Yeah, it's worth it. . . . God has a plan for me.

Three o'clock, a hot August night, and I couldn't tear myself away from the computer. The article, "A Soldier's Plea," written by Sgt. James Martin, doing combat duty in Iraq, brought me close to tears. James, an Army medic, wrote of how difficult it was to be far from his wife and two kids, and yet, helping to save an Iraqi soldier's infant son changed him in a way he didn't know was possible. When the war began, he was a single parent. He could have deferred, let another medic go in his place. I couldn't imagine making the choice he did. *He's sacrificing so much,* I thought, *to help protect people he doesn't even know. To protect all of us.*

War stories were not my usual bedtime reading. As a single mother and writer living in New York City, my world could hardly be more different from the one James lived in. I had great respect for the military—my mom emigrated from the Philippines after US troops liberated that nation from Japanese occupation during World War II—but I never thought about their sacrifice. Not really. Not like this.

I was thinking only about my four-year-old, Sofia, the morning I took her to see the USS *Intrepid,* a famous World War II–era aircraft carrier anchored in the Hudson River on the West Side of Manhattan that now serves as a museum. Sofia was going through a shark phase—everything from her picture books and bath toys to her favorite T-shirt had to have sharks on it—and I'd heard about a fighter jet painted with shark's teeth on the *Intrepid's* flight deck. Sofia was so excited to see it.

We took some photos with the jet, then headed belowdecks. A video showed black-and-white footage of the ship under attack. To my right, an elderly gentleman leaned on a cane. "I was there that day," he whispered. "I was there."

The video ended and a group gathered around the veteran. "Do you see that man?" I asked Sofia. She nodded. I explained that he had protected our family during a war many years ago.

"We should thank him," I said.

Sofia walked up to the circle of adults. I'd begun to think I had made a mistake when the man finally turned to her and asked, "What can I do for you, little girl?"

"Thank you for being brave on the boat," Sofia said. "I like your boat!"

Everyone went silent. The man's eyes filled with tears. An older woman pulled me aside. "Thank you for her words," she said. "You have no idea how much they mean to my husband. This is his last visit to the ship."

The look in the old sailor's eyes stayed with me as I tried to sleep that night. If it weren't for people like him, my mom would never have made it to this country. Sofia and I wouldn't be here.

You have no idea how much her words mean. What about our soldiers serving today? How could I let them know that I was grateful for what they did? I got out of bed, sat at my computer and did a search.

After a few clicks I found something: "Adopt a US Soldier." That sounded interesting. All it required was sending one letter a week and a care package every month. Sofia and I could do it together. I signed up.

But I knew nothing about what our soldiers were going through. What could I say in my letters? I did another search, this one for their stories. Among millions of results, James's article stood out. It was so moving.

I kept his words in mind as I dove into caring for my adopted soldier. I'd been assigned a staff sergeant deployed to the mountains of eastern Afghanistan. His wife had recently given birth to their first child, a baby boy, so along with my letters I sent him a copy of the book *What to Expect the First Year*. I wanted to make sure he could be an active daddy even from afar. Sofia helped me pick out the candy and other treats to ship to him, and stuck stamps on the letters.

By Christmas, I felt a strong urge to do more. I couldn't adopt a second soldier—I was only one person—but I found another program, called Cup of Joe. For only two dollars, I could send a randomly selected service member a hot cup of coffee and a personal e-mail—a small taste of comfort from home. I sent twenty cups to different soldiers, along with messages of gratitude: "What I really want to give you for Christmas is the certainty that you are not forgotten. Sincerely, Gina."

One soldier immediately wrote back to me.

"Gina, that was about the sweetest sentiment I have ever received," he said. "I will copy this and save it for Christmases in the future. May this message find you with happiness, love, and always security. Warmest of regards, Jim."

I replied, telling him a funny Sofia anecdote and mentioning my work as a writer. He quickly responded. "Writing's always been a dream of mine. In fact, I even got something published once. Check it out...."

I clicked the link he sent. *Today I sit in Iraq, my family and loved ones in America....* Wait a minute.

It was "A Soldier's Plea" by Sgt. James Martin. That was Jim, one deployed soldier out of thousands, who had received my random cup of coffee. Or was it random? My hands shook as I typed a response. "Jim, you have no idea how much your words meant to me...."

Jim and I still keep in touch by e-mail. He's back home, working for the VA, and I've started a blog, "Gina Left the Mall," about connecting with our troops. My life has changed so much since that sleepless August night when our paths crossed. One article among millions, meant for me to find.

OUR ZACKARY
by Kristy Miklas

I had given up. A third child wasn't possible. I told myself that my husband, Carl, and I should be grateful for the two we had. We were richly blessed. But still I couldn't stop feeling that a part of our family was missing, that for some reason we needed to keep trying, to keep searching.

Our daughter, Kelly, was born early in our marriage. Then, after a long struggle with infertility (and at great expense), we adopted a son, Anthony, domestically. At that point we didn't have enough money to adopt again or try for another child, and yet I yearned for one! *Forgive me, Lord,* I prayed, *for wanting more than You have already given.*

My aunt Sandra, my dad's sister and the family genealogist, thought the urge was familial. "Your great-great-grandfather was one of fifteen siblings back in Lithuania," she told me. "We Lithuanians love big families!"

Then came a call that my paternal grandfather's brother, Tony Litvin, had died. I hardly knew Uncle Tony. He lived far away, traveled little. He'd never met our kids, or known about our struggles. But he'd died childless and wanted to leave something for future generations. "He gave you a small inheritance," Aunt Sandra told us.

"Maybe it's a sign that we could find another child," I said to Carl. A child who, I felt, was waiting for us.

"You should adopt from Russia," we heard. "You won't have to wait as long." I admit I hesitated. Lithuania had suffered terribly under Russian oppression. "The past is past," I told myself. "We can't blame the children, only love them."

In less than a year we were matched up with an eight-month-old boy. Our adoption coordinator sent a video. As soon as Carl came home from work, we sat down and watched. What a beautiful little boy! He took my breath—and my heart—away. But there was something odd about the label on the box.

I called the coordinator. "The name on the box. You made a mistake."

"No," she said, "that's the child's name. Denis Litvin."

"Denis, yes," I clarified. "But I'm Miklas now, not Litvin. Litvin is my maiden name."

"It's also the child's name," the woman insisted. "Denis Litvin."

Our son's birth parents were Litvins? In Russia? How could that be? I didn't know what to think.

We flew to Russia and sat through a court session, waiting for the stone-faced judge to finalize the adoption. We'd heard horror stories about couples traveling so many miles, falling in love with their child, and being told at the last minute that no, it couldn't be because of some legal snarl or bureaucratic foul-up.

All at once the judge smiled. Her interpreter translated. "I've never seen this before. Your maiden name—it's the same as the child's. Of course your adoption is approved."

We gave our son the name Zackary, and brought him home to meet his new family. Aunt Sandra couldn't get over how closely he resembled my younger brother, Rob, when he was little. "They are practically identical," she gasped.

"Well, he *is* a Litvin," I joked, and told Aunt Sandra about the coincidence of our name.

Aunt Sandra looked at me, awestruck. "Did you know," she said slowly, "one of your great-great-grandfather's brothers emigrated to Russia? No one's heard from that branch of the family since." *Until now,* I thought.

We haven't done a DNA test yet. Our son's birth parents remain a mystery. But it matters little. Zackary has a family now, a large, loving one, and a mom and dad and two siblings who are thrilled to have him. We were called to have another child—*this* child. He was waiting for us, waiting to join his family.

THE CASE OF THE RED CARNATIONS
by Peg Golda Getty

I stood at the microphone, a bouquet of red carnations clutched in my hand, pulling my thoughts together. I was trying to find the right words to share the secret I'd kept for years—the key to a decades-old mystery. I was back in Jordan, Minnesota, where I'd grown up, the scene of a tragedy that changed my life and the lives of many others. They didn't talk about the accident much, but the people of this small, devout town had never forgotten my sister, Judy.

I was only eight years old that terrible night. Judy was seventeen, a junior in high school. I idolized her. She was one of the stars—the class president, an artist, drummer in the school band, honor-roll student. She'd been at dress rehearsal for the class play that evening and everybody went to get something to eat. Nine kids piled into one vehicle. Too many. A tractor trailer plowed into the back of the car. Five of the students were critically injured. Two were killed, including Judy.

I thought my parents would never get over it; I thought I never would. A quiet sadness pervaded our home. Life moved on but the grief stayed. I thought no one else could understand how we felt. We went to the cemetery often. Dad weeded the plot, Mom brushed off the gravestone. The dates engraved in it were of a life cut short: 1939–1956. "Hey, sis," I'd whisper, "I miss you so much."

Some of Judy's friends looked out for me, even tried to fill her big-sister role. Her friend Mary led my Girl Scout troop and took me on my first canoe trip in the wilderness. She encouraged me in my tomboy ways. I grew to love Mary. She was so much like my sister. But not even she could replace Judy.

Then came the red carnations. The first Memorial Day after Judy's death, my parents and I visited the cemetery, as always, just to be close to her. We walked to the grave under the tree. There on the stone lay a bouquet of a dozen red carnations—her class flower. No note, no indication of who put them there, just the flowers, brilliant against the flinty headstone. *Someone else understands,* I thought. *Someone who loved my sister as much as I did.*

Every Memorial Day after that, the flowers mysteriously appeared. Life moved on, but someone remembered our loss. Someone still wanted to comfort us. Who?

I was determined to figure it out. I questioned Judy's friends. I talked about it at school. No one knew who could be leaving the flowers. Or would admit to it. One night my high-school boyfriend and I hid in the cemetery, sure we would discover the secret mourner. We waited as late as we could. We didn't see a soul. *This year there won't be any flowers,* I thought. But the next morning the red carnations were there.

I went to college and married a great guy named Bruce. I became a phys-ed teacher and girls' coach. Bruce and I had a family. Sometimes we made it back to Jordan for Memorial Day and I'd go with Mom and Dad to the cemetery to see those red carnations sitting reassuringly, comfortingly, anonymously, on top of Judy's grave. After all those years, it had become the biggest mystery in town. No one ever caught the giver of the carnations in the act. Everyone had theories—a heartbroken admirer, the guilt-stricken trucker, a ghost, even. In the end I decided that if God had wanted me to know, he would have told me.

Then one year I was at a coaching clinic at Bemidji State University the Tuesday after Memorial Day. In a packed gym I took a seat next to another girls' coach. I introduced myself and she asked me where I was from. "Jordan," I said. "It's a small town. You probably wouldn't have heard of it."

"Jordan?" she exclaimed. "I was just there! What a sweet little town. But I'm exhausted. I was visiting this friend. She made me stay up with her until the middle of the night so she could sneak into a cemetery and put a dozen red carnations on someone's grave."

Carnations? The blood must have drained from my face. "Who was your friend?" I asked.

"You've got to promise you won't tell anyone," she said. "She doesn't want anyone to know. Not while she's alive, at least."

I made that promise. I kept it for years, only confiding in Bruce. Then one night, he was scrolling through the online edition of my old hometown paper, something he rarely did. After all, Mom and Dad had died years earlier and we had moved away to Idaho. All at once, Bruce looked up and said, "You need to go back to Jordan."

There was a memorial service, fifty-six years after my sister's, that I had to attend, because I had a secret I could finally share. That's why I was here, standing before a microphone with a bouquet of red carnations in my hand. The hall was packed with nearly three hundred people grieving the loss of so much: a mother, a wife, a teacher, a friend. Mary. My sister's friend, the girl who had done so much for me after Judy died.

"Most of you know a lot about Mary," I said. "What a great coach she was, a great teacher. She inspired me to become a coach and teacher myself. But she also did something extraordinary you may not know...."

I finished my story and not a soul moved in the hall. Then people stood and clapped. Some came up and hugged me. Judy's old classmates, Mary's friends and family.

I looked at the flowers in my hand. I'd originally thought I'd put them on Mary's grave. But not now. They needed to go someplace else.

I found the old cemetery looking much the same. I stopped at the stone of a girl who had died too young. I brushed it off just as Mom had, weeded around it as Dad always did, then put down the bouquet, as Mary would have wanted. It was an act of love, a tradition—one that I would now continue.

A FRIEND IN NEED
by Marion Wilson

For most kids, having a friend switch schools wouldn't be a disaster. My son, Steve, though, is different.

His friend Chris's mom knew as much when she called one night to tell me she would be sending her son to private school for his junior year the following September. I tried to sound cheerful but I was devastated. *God, don't let this happen to Steve. Not again,* I thought. *Not after what happened with John.*

Folks had barely heard of Asperger's when Steve was younger. I certainly hadn't. Until he was diagnosed, I couldn't understand why he was so laser-focused reading a book, but couldn't look anyone in the eye, much less hold a two-way conversation. He could rattle off the statistics of the entire Chicago Cubs lineup, but ignored directions in the classroom and found it difficult to work in a group. He struggled to connect with other kids his age. Asperger's has no cure, but knowing the diagnosis helped, in some ways. At least now we understood why Steve was so introverted. It wasn't his fault—or ours. In third grade we signed him up for Little League, hoping his love of baseball would help him fit in with his team.

It wasn't until fifth grade that he came into his own. Assigned a group project on Native Americans, Steve discovered that he had a lot in common with the other boys in his group, Chris and John. Chris loved baseball as much as Steve did, while John, with his big heart and contagious laughter, charmed Steve instantly.

The boys began to spend time together outside of school, going to the movies, playing catch. A friendship developed between them, and a side of Steve emerged that I'd never seen before. One that was comfortable just being who he was.

For his twelfth birthday, Steve invited John and Chris to sleep over. We ordered pizza and turned the living room over to the boys. They played video games and watched movies. Steve's laughter echoed throughout the house, traveling all the way upstairs to my bedroom. I couldn't help but sneak a peek—the boys were on the couch, mashing buttons on their game controllers and joking around about the battle taking place on-screen. Steve was so natural—he had finally found friends who loved him. Better, who *accepted* him. Perhaps in a way only the mother of such a child could know, it was a kind of miracle, an answer to prayer.

Then John came to us with the news. He was going to go live with his father in Ohio. Steve didn't talk for days. I was heartbroken too. The boys kept in touch at first, but one day Steve called and reached a recorded message. John's cell phone had been disconnected. *His family's going through a tough transition,* I thought. *He'll reach out when he can.* We hadn't heard from him in well over a year.

At least Steve had had Chris. Now Chris would be moving on too.

"We want Steve to be okay," Chris's mother told me. "That's why I called. I thought it would be better if Steve heard the news from you first."

I did my best to sound composed. "We'll be fine," I said. "Chris's new school will be so lucky to have him." We arranged to catch up over coffee the next week and said good-bye.

I hung up, feeling hopeless. I dreaded telling Steve. It'd been hard enough to lose John. Now he would be all alone, would sink back into isolation. How could God let this happen?

The next morning, Steve came downstairs for breakfast with hair a bit tousled from sleep, but he looked well rested and peaceful. I hated to do this. But it was better he learn the news here, where I could console him.

"Steve, there's something you need to know," I began. I told him about Chris.

Steve stared ahead silently for a long minute. The painful news hung in the air. What was going on inside his head?

He blinked. "That's okay," he finally said. "We'll still see each other some, I bet." I searched his face. He looked like he really meant it. "It'll be okay," he said again. I planted a kiss on his forehead before clearing the dishes.

I'd underestimated my son.

We spent a quiet afternoon at home, watching one of Steve's favorite history movies, *Flags of Our Fathers*. He called Chris and learned all about the new school he would be attending. "They've got a great baseball team," he told me.

I gave my boy a hug. Maybe this wasn't exactly the answer to my prayer, but it was making me feel better about the situation. He was handling it, as if he really did know that things would be all right.

I was just getting dinner ready when the phone rang again. My heart raced. *What now?*

"Hi there," said a friendly voice I couldn't quite place.

"Hello. Who is this?" I asked.

"It's me—John!"

"John!" I exclaimed, ecstatic.

Steve grabbed the phone. Soon he began to laugh—the same laughter that had filled the house during his birthday sleepover. I left the room to give him some privacy. I couldn't believe it! A call from John was just what Steve needed right now.

"Mom!" Steve shouted. He dropped the phone without hanging up, so excited he could hardly contain himself. "Guess what? John and his dad are moving back here!"

The day before, a phone call shook my faith in Steve and in God. Just twenty-four hours later, another phone call brought it all back. I'll never stop worrying about Steve—I am a mother, after all. He may be a little different from other kids. But now I know he will never be alone either.

OFF COURSE?

by Paul Stutzman

The wind gently combing through the rust-colored weeds, calm waves lapping at the hull of my yellow kayak. Peaceful, right? Wrong. I didn't want to spend one more minute on this stinkin' river out in the middle of nowhere. I swatted another mosquito. I was tired of muttering to the empty air, sick of complaining, sick of being alone. Sick of *myself.*

Ever since my wife, Mary, died, seven years earlier, I'd been searching for something I couldn't quite describe. I'd quit my job as a restaurant manager to hike the Appalachian Trail, more than two thousand miles. Then I'd biked five thousand miles from Washington State to Florida. All by myself.

Alone was not the way we did things where I came from. I grew up in a traditional Mennonite family. My three sisters' idea of getting away from it all was the cross-country bus trip with thirty of our cousins that they were on right now. I needed to be with family, they said. No thank you. As much as I adored my family, they were smothering me. Stopping by with enough casseroles to feed an army, calling daily to check up on me.

I hadn't yet found what I was looking for, but I wasn't going to find it with them, whatever it was. Closure? Peace? Understanding? God?

I'd wanted to paddle down the Mississippi to the Gulf of Mexico ever since reading *Adventures of Huckleberry Finn* as a kid. I bought all the guidebooks, did the research, mapped out my route. Most kayakers finished in three months. I would do it in two. Sure, the first leg of the journey, in northern Minnesota, would be tricky. But I could manage it.

Wrong. I'd spent the first day stuck in weeds, forced to carry my kayak over my head in search of deeper water. Next came muddy swamps, channels clogged with fallen trees, wild-rice fields so tall and packed it was like trying to paddle through a hairbrush. Then I flipped my kayak, landing headfirst in the roaring river and soaking my cell phone. It hadn't worked since.

Now I was nearing a dot labeled Cohasset on the map, north of Grand Rapids. Not on my original route. In fact, I should've been in Iowa by now. But I was too exhausted to correct my course. "Lord, I want to go home!" I cried out. Eight days—that's how long it'd taken the mighty Mississippi to finally break a tough old guy like me.

What had I been trying to prove? I'd come out here to be alone, and I'd gotten my wish. I couldn't even call anyone.

I spotted Cohasset in the distance. A desolate beach. I wondered what I'd find on shore. Bears? Coyotes? A plague of locusts?

My pocket vibrated. My phone? I grabbed it, hands trembling. The screen glowed. How was it working?

"Paul? Paul?" the voice on the other end crackled. My brother-in-law? Wasn't he on the big bus trip?

"I had the strangest urge to call you," he said. "You okay out there?"

"I dunno," I admitted. "Honestly, it's been a nightmare. What about you? How's the West Coast?"

"We took a bit of a detour through Canada," he said. "We're headed back. You in Iowa yet?"

"Not yet," I said, sitting up straighter in my kayak. "Where are you?"

"Let me check with the driver," he said. "Looks like we're about to pass through some tiny town . . . Cohasset, Minnesota. Ever heard of it?"

A tiny dot on the map. A tiny dot where my kayak had been pulled. A place where I found myself asking, had I been carried here by the mighty Mississippi? Or something mightier? Had I really been alone?

I hung up and paddled to shore. Soon I was sitting on a warm, spacious bus with my brother-in-law, three sisters, and thirty cousins. Exactly where I finally knew I needed to be.

SOMEWHERE IN QUITO
by Woody Gimbel

Out of nowhere the butterfly flitted across the path, lingered on a flower, darted up into the sky, then came back down to us. Iridescent wings catching the sunshine, dazzling with color. Ally followed it and we followed Ally.

We were in the Botanical Gardens in Quito, Ecuador, 9,350 feet above sea level, the snow-dusted Andes encircling us. Clouds hung over the mountains and a brilliant rainbow pierced the canopy. I should have been happy, here on vacation with my wife, Carol. We had flown in to visit our oldest son, Sam, and his friend Ally, but an uneasiness hovered over me. Why was Sam here? Why couldn't he get on with his life and go to medical school as we had planned? Why this aimless choice by a kid who normally kept his nose to the grindstone? I had always trusted him. Now I wasn't so sure.

On our flight from Virginia I shared my feelings with Carol. "Why does Sam need to backpack through the Andes for months, 'finding himself,' when he never seemed lost in the first place?" He'd aced his pre-med curriculum and graduated near the top of his class. He was a shoo-in for med school.

"Think about what you were like at his age," Carol had said.

Well, yes, but Sam wasn't me. My buddies and I at the University of Virginia partied hard, but kids did in those days, didn't they? The class of 1966 had Vietnam hanging over our heads. We had to let off steam. Some nights we tore a hole in the morning and crawled right through. The wildest of us, our crazy leader, was Chuck. He was studying to be a doctor, but you wouldn't know it watching him drive his Harley along the campus sidewalks, laughing and shouting as if he hadn't a care in the world. That was Chuck.

"Times were different," I said. "I didn't know what I wanted to do." I went straight into the military after school. Served for four years, went to grad school, got busy with marriage, kids, work. As for Chuck, I thought of him as a cautionary tale—he'd dropped off the face of the earth. Sam seemed headed for great things. I didn't want him to get lost, to blow his chances like Chuck and others had.

"I've been praying for the right words to say to him," I told Carol.

Sam met us at the airport with Ally. She was a free spirit, the one who had encouraged his newfound wanderlust. I had suspected that she was a bad influence, but I liked her right away—polite and self-possessed. And Sam, he'd changed, grown. I could tell immediately. He was more sure of himself, confident but not rebellious. His Spanish was good enough to get us through the throng of taxi drivers and safely to our hotel.

The next morning we visited the local market, toured the old colonial quarter, straddled the equator, ate excellent ceviche. No chance for a heart-to-heart with my son. Today, at the Botanical Gardens, I hoped there'd be a moment when I could talk some sense into him. He'd had his fun. Now it was time to get serious.

We wandered along the garden paths, admiring a tree here, a cactus there. Sam took a picture of the rainbow. "Look!" Ally gasped. I saw that vibration of color, the butterfly, almost as if it had been spun off by the rainbow. Ally dashed after it.

We followed her zigzag path. It seemed as aimless as this trip of Sam's. Chasing after butterflies. Chasing after vague notions of the future. I lagged several paces behind, feeling light-headed in the thin atmosphere. The butterfly led us to a bridge over a koi pond, then vanished into the sky. Catching my breath, I barely noticed the man sitting at a table there, book in hand. But he and Carol began to talk. "Where are you from?" I heard him ask in English.

"Charlottesville, Virginia," Carol answered. He put down his book. "I went to school at the University of Virginia," he said. "Class of sixty-six."

I stared at him. In an instant the years dropped away. The same crooked grin, the piercing eyes... I could picture him raising Cain on his old Harley. "Chuck?" I exclaimed.

"Woody?" he said.

We hugged, pounding each other on the back. "Sam, this is my old buddy Chuck, from college," I said. I fought off my sense of disbelief. Chuck? Here? In Quito, of all places? The five of us sat down. There was so much catching up to do. We laughed at the things we had done back in the day, shook our heads as if we still couldn't believe it.

"You know," Chuck said, "I wasn't as carefree back then as I wanted everyone to think. I was a pretty unhappy kid."

I thought of that conversation I wanted to have with Sam. "Did you end up going to med school?" I asked.

"Nope," Chuck said. "I finally realized it wasn't really what I wanted to do. It was my father's plan. So I traveled and tried to find out what I did want. Met a beautiful woman and we settled here. Life has been good to me."

I stayed silent. "I was planning on going to med school too," Sam said, "but I don't think I'd be happy being a doctor."

Not happy? What did being happy have to do with it? Chuck looked at him. "Only you can decide what's right for you, the path that is most likely to make you happy. I'm glad I finally found mine."

All at once I knew. I too had found my path. I was happy with the way my life had turned out and suddenly very proud of my adventurous son. I knew what I needed to say to Sam, not right now, but soon enough: "I love you. I only want you to be happy. Whatever you choose to do."

Three years have flown by since the day a butterfly led me to that reunion in the least likely of places. Chuck and I still keep in touch, telling old stories and new ones. Sam returned to the States and found another career—developing software. He's doing very well. He's happy, even if I don't understand a thing about computers or what he does. I trust him.

I trust something else too, now more than ever. No matter where our paths in life take us, our steps are guided, even by a butterfly that seems to emerge from a rainbow.

LOST HEIRLOOMS

by Mary Hayes Calhoun Owings

Life didn't start out easy for me, growing up in South Carolina during the peak of the Great Depression. My mother passed away when I was twelve. My father couldn't care for my brother and me and still make a living, so I was sent to live with one of my aunts while my brother was sent to live with another. Our home was sold, with nearly all of my mother's precious belongings scattered.

I'm ninety-two now. I've built my own family with four children—three girls and a boy—and fourteen grandchildren and great-grandchildren. My husband passed away a few years ago, and my children live in South Carolina, two here in Laurens. I keep up a tradition my husband and I started inviting neighbors and friends over for five o'clock coffee and conversation, and often have my girlfriends visit for lunch. I am so grateful and full of love for aunts, uncles, and friends who shared their homes with me.

Even so, after eighty years, I still can't get through a Mother's Day without wishing my mother hadn't been taken so soon. A visit to an antique shop will make me wistful—a mirror, a monogrammed card case, a cologne bottle, a set of china sparking memories of the short time we had together.

Recently, I visited my daughter Dee for a long weekend. One morning, as we lingered over a second cup of coffee, Dee told me that she had a gift for me. "My mother-in-law bought some china from an estate sale in Pennsylvania," she said. "It matches my décor, but there are only four luncheon plates, four soup bowls, and one bread-and-butter plate, so I wouldn't use it. I thought you might like it since you admire antiques."

"Oh, thanks! Let's see the china," I said.

Dee brought it out. White plates with pink, yellow, and blue bunches of flowers in the middle and around the circumference. The gold leaf edges were worn with age. I'd only seen china with that pattern once before.

I picked up one of the plates and held it gently, running my fingers over the gold leaf. "How—how did you know?" I asked softly.

"Know what, Mom?"

"Dee," I said, "this was my mother's china."

CHAPTER 6

All Things Become New

BIG RED
by Jill Davis

So this is what the end feels like. I stared out the window of my parents' living room. The sun shone brightly, but I couldn't feel its warmth. The light felt harsh and unforgiving. Winter's typical days—cold, gray, overcast—had been slow to arrive that December in southern Missouri, but I was in a kind of darkness, lost in my own personal blizzard. I could barely find the will to get out of bed. I didn't see the point.

I'd been here a month, mostly staying in my room, blinds closed, or wandering the house like a ghost. Daddy had brought me home from New York City. I'd moved there with big dreams. At twenty-five, I'd been accepted into a writing program. But the city was so fast, so busy, so loud, like no place I'd ever lived. I couldn't stay focused. A harsh review by a professor sent me spiraling downward into a sadness that never lifted. Finally, I checked into a hospital. "Clinical depression," the doctor said. The call home was so hard to make. I felt like a failure.

Daddy looked up from the book he was reading, a thin smile on his face. "Honey, you feeling okay?" he asked. I knew he was trying to help. But it felt like my parents were constantly hovering. I needed to get away from their worried expressions.

I looked out at the sun again. An urge struck me. I should go outside. "Guess I'll take a walk," I mumbled.

I opened the front door. The light nearly blinded me. I felt something at my side. A big, beautiful Irish setter had bounded over from next door. I didn't know the neighbors had a dog. I shuffled down the driveway. The dog loped along beside me. His coat shone, thick and lustrous. He was lean, but not skinny. Definitely well cared for. Strong.

My legs felt like dead weight. I forced myself to walk, each step an effort. My parents lived on a circular road a half-mile long. The houses were set back from the street, with spacious yards. In the distance I could see the woods and farm fields I'd explored growing up. Once they'd meant joy and freedom.

"What am I supposed to do now?" I said out loud, to no one.

The dog cocked his head at the sound of my voice. His gaze was piercing, focused. I had his undivided attention.

"How could I have been so stupid?" I asked him. How ludicrous was it that I was conversing with an Irish setter? Yet I plowed on. "I don't even know who I am anymore, what I'm good at. I can't just live here with Mom and Dad forever."

The setter ran off behind a nearby tree, sniffing the ground intently. I took a deep breath and walked on. *Great,* I thought, *I can't even hold a dog's attention.*

I cut across a field to the woods and reached an overgrown path. There was the dog again. He had beaten me here somehow. *Fast,* I thought. "What's your name?" I asked. He looked up and swished his tail. "I'm going to call you Big Red."

We walked for miles. I don't know how I found the energy. Finally, we reached a park. I sat at a picnic table and held my head in my hands, dazed with exhaustion. Something soft rubbed against my leg. Big Red. I scratched behind his ears.

"Don't you have anything better to do than hang out with me?" I said. "Your owner is probably out looking for you. We'd better head back."

He followed me home, occasionally streaking off to chase a squirrel. He was so full of life! At the door he broke away from me and sat calmly in the neighbor's yard, looking at me, panting softly. He was just a dog, but there was something inexplicably reassuring about him.

At dinner I asked Daddy if he had seen the neighbor's big red setter before.

"No," he said, puzzling over the question. "Never. They're not dog people. Don't think anyone around here owns a setter."

"Odd," I said. "He's magnificent."

The next day I opened the door to take out the trash, a monumental task for me. I almost fell over Big Red. He wagged his tail. "I don't feel like walking today," I told him. But he wouldn't go away. "Fine," I said. "You win."

Leaves crunched beneath my feet and his paws. I told him how lonely I was. Would I meet someone special? Ever get married? Who would love a failure like me? Big Red gazed up at me with his dark, searching eyes. He never made a sound. Nice to have a listener who never judged me. I told him everything, my deepest worries and insecurities. Things I'd never told anyone. Things I needed to get out, like a poison, my fears and self-doubt.

Big Red greeted me every morning that winter. We walked for hours. I began to observe him intently. Every outing seemed like a new adventure to him, a beautiful day full of possibilities. But where had he come from? Where did he go at night? I never fed him, never did anything to entice him to stay with me. Yet suddenly he would appear, as if from thin air, and disappear the same way.

Big Red wasn't the only unusual thing about that winter. It was unseasonably warm. The sun was as constant as my canine companion. I began to feel stronger. I noticed the sound of the river babbling over rocks. The excited way Big Red wagged his tail when he spied a bird. And at long last I felt something reawaken within me, a spark of life, a pinpoint of light to lead me from my darkness. The pain and the doubt, the hurt of rejection started to fade, the way a bruise fades, and I felt my soul heal.

I accepted a job at a law firm in Texas. On my last day in Missouri, I knelt down and hugged Big Red tight. "Thanks for everything," I said.

"I'm going to miss you." He jogged over to the yard where I'd first seen him and lay down.

After a few weeks I called my parents to say I was doing well. "How's Big Red?" I asked.

"Wish I knew," Daddy said. "Right after you left that dog took off. Your mom thinks he came from heaven. But I told her strays have a way of disappearing."

THE RECOVERY
by Kelli Tipton

It was an ordinary Bible, worn at the edges, with a plain blue cover. On the front, embossed in gold lettering, was my brother's name: Langdon Horn. It was the Bible he'd taken with him to rehab. The Bible he'd relied on to get clean and sober.

Then it disappeared, and I worried my brother's sobriety might vanish with it.

I'd never known the worst of Langdon's struggles. He hid his problems well. He didn't share the painful details of his divorce with me or the rest of the family. Didn't confide in anyone how he coped with being separated from his two daughters, Alex and Arden, who lived with their mother seventy miles away, in Anniston, Alabama. He filled the absence with drugs.

"Langdon didn't want anyone to know the real truth," Mom told me the day my brother checked himself into the rehabilitation facility.

I knew how hard it must have been for him to seek help, and I was proud of him for taking that step. But shaking the habit meant opening up, not holding everything in. It was about confiding in others and trusting completely in a higher power. I'd never known my brother to do that.

The Bible was the first thing Langdon showed me when I visited him in rehab.

"I highlighted the verses I rely on the most for strength. It's my spiritual road map to recovery," he said. I flipped through the pages. They were covered in notes and he had underlined passages that seemed to speak to him directly. Inside that little blue book were all the secret struggles Langdon hadn't wanted anyone to see. I might never know the whole of Langdon's story, but his Bible held the truth.

Langdon completed treatment and returned home, bringing the Bible with him. It was comforting for him to think of it always beside him when he needed it. The three months he had spent out of work had left many bills unpaid—and Langdon didn't have the cash to cover them. He lost his phone service and struggled to buy food. Somehow, he kept it together. He made a little money working construction.

Then one day I got a phone call. Langdon sounded despondent. His truck had been repossessed. But he didn't care about the truck. He cared about what was in the truck. His Bible.

"I can't believe it's gone!" Langdon said. "I'd forgotten that I'd left it on the front seat."

"Can you find out where it was towed?" I asked.

"I tried," he said. "Somewhere in Birmingham, but it was auctioned off—along with everything in it. The Bible's gone."

His Bible. His road map to recovery, I thought.

Langdon bought himself another Bible, although I worried that it could never mean as much to him as the one that had guided him through those early, dark days. He had lost so much! But he got right on with rebuilding his life. He found a regular construction job, which helped him pay his bills, including child support for Alex and Arden. The girls spent every other weekend with him. He made it to the one-year mark.

"I still miss that Bible," he admitted to me. "But it's God's Word that's most important."

Recovery was a daily struggle for Langdon, as it is for many addicts. I watched him closely over the course of the next few years. And I prayed every day for the Lord to guide and protect him.

It had been five years since my brother left rehab when I went to his house one Saturday morning. It was his turn to have Alex and Arden for the weekend, and he was looking forward to seeing them. When the girls arrived they wrapped their arms around him in a group hug.

"We have something for you, Dad," Alex said. *Dad*. It was amazing what five sober years had done for his relationship with his daughters.

"You got me something?" Langdon said. "You didn't have to. It's not my birthday."

The girls grinned at each other. "It's actually from Grandma," said Arden. "She was at her church in Anniston, going through the donation box, and found something she thought you should have. She made us promise to give it to you right away."

Alex and Arden handed him the gift. An ordinary Bible, worn at the edges, with a plain blue cover. Embossed in gold lettering on the front cover was my brother's name: LANGDON HORN. Page after page was filled with notes and underlining, in the shaky hand of a man starting out on the road to new life.

THE INTERSECTION
by Brett Bainter

The only one I blamed more than God was myself. What kind of father would let something like this happen to his little boy? It didn't matter how much everyone, especially my wife, Jodi, tried to reassure me, "It wasn't your fault, Brett. It was an accident." Yes, it was an accident. And I was the one who'd caused it.

If only I'd heard my son, we wouldn't be here in St. Petersburg on this February morning. We would be back home in Orlando, dropping Jake off at school, watching him dash down the sidewalk to join his friends. Instead, I drove slowly through downtown St. Pete even though we had an appointment to keep. It wasn't the traffic—the streets were quiet for a Tuesday morning. And I knew the way—we'd made this two-hour drive from our house in Orlando countless times since that terrible afternoon four years earlier. I guess part of me wanted to put off the inevitable, if only for a few minutes.

I glanced in the rearview mirror at my son in the backseat. From this angle Jake looked like a typical eight-year-old boy—short sandy hair, gaps in his smile where permanent teeth were growing in, skinny but sturdy, sleepy-eyed from having to get up early. Except he wasn't like other kids. He'd been through so much these past four years—pain so excruciating he needed morphine, tissue and bone transplants, sixteen surgeries. Walking was a struggle for him. Running and riding a bike, impossible.

Jake had held up like a champ, braver than any little boy should ever have to be. Yet sometimes I'd catch a hint of sadness in his eyes at everything he had to miss out on. All because of me.

My guilt had kept the memory of that day fresh, like some kind of psychic preservative. April 9, 2004. Jodi was at work. I was working in my home office. Jake was three, about to turn four. If there was one thing that defined him, it was motion. He'd walked at eleven months and we'd barely been able to keep up with him since. He was zipping up and down the driveway on his training bike, a babysitter watching him.

I got done with business early so I decided to cut the grass. I hopped on the riding mower and cut the front lawn. I waved to Jake as I drove around back. *Pretty soon he won't need those training wheels.*

I was backing up the mower when I felt a bump underneath. What did I hit? I turned, looked down. A small blond head and skinny upper body were sticking out from under the mower. *Jake! Oh, God, no!*

Somehow I lifted the mower off my son. Our next-door neighbor, a nurse, worked on stopping the bleeding until the ambulance got there.

I called Jodi, crying so hard I could barely get the words out to explain what happened. "I've done the worst thing a dad could ever do."

The right side of Jake's right leg and the smaller toes on his foot were gone, sliced off by the powerful mower blade. We tried everything to repair his leg. But four years of surgeries, braces, and physical therapy pointed to one inescapable conclusion: Jake's leg would never work properly. His damaged knee wouldn't bend. The bones in his lower leg grew wrong, angling away from his body.

Jodi brought it up first. She was braver than I. "There's one option we haven't considered," she said. "Amputation." I didn't want to even talk about it. If Jake didn't have a whole leg, how could he have a whole life?

But Jodi persisted. We consulted specialists all over the country. Finally Jodi asked a surgeon point-blank: Would our son be better off with a prosthetic limb? The answer was yes.

That was why we were in St. Petersburg now, on our way to All Children's Hospital, where a surgical team would amputate my son's right leg above the knee.

The worst thing a dad could ever do. Jodi kept trying to get me to think differently. "It wasn't your fault," she said. "Jake jumped off his bike and ran after you too fast for anyone to stop him." Our son's ordeal had driven her to find solace and draw strength from prayer, but all it did for me was confirm my guilt. How could God let me run over my son and ruin his leg and his life? No loving God, I thought, would allow such a senseless thing to happen to an innocent child.

We came to a stoplight at the intersection of Third Street and Sixth Avenue. I couldn't help but think we were at some sort of crossroads in our lives. Should we go ahead with the surgery? We lived on a lake and Jake loved exploring outside, learning about fish and ducks and nature. Would he lose all that when he lost his leg? Jodi and I had talked it over endlessly. Jodi had prayed. Jake didn't seem fazed when we told him. Still, we were making the decision for him. How could we be sure we were doing the right thing?

The only other people on the street were a group of three bicyclists approaching the intersection, slowing down. The light turned green and I started to pull away. Out of the corner of my eye I saw the rider in the middle lose his balance. He veered toward the curb and half-slipped, half-fell from his bike. He tugged at his foot. His friends finally pried his shoe loose from the pedal clip.

Suddenly Jake piped up. "Hey, that guy on the bike has a fake leg!" I looked. The cyclist who'd fallen…was that a glint of metal on his leg?

I turned the car around, pulled up to the cyclists and hopped out. Jodi and Jake got out too. Now that we were close I could see that the man sitting on the curb wore a prosthesis below his right knee. He was shaking his head, muttering something. Then he looked up and saw us.

"We're the Bainters," I said. "Brett, Jodi, and this little guy here is Jake." I blurted, "He's on his way to the hospital to have his leg amputated."

The man studied us for a moment through his sunglasses, his gaze going to the brace on Jake's leg. I thought, *That must have sounded weird.*

Then he got up effortlessly from the curb. "Hey, I'm Bill," he said in a gruff voice. He was maybe in his sixties, fit and muscular. He walked over to Jake and stuck out his hand. "You're probably a little nervous right now," he said. "Don't be. Once you have your surgery and get your new leg, you'll be in great shape. Look at me."

Jake couldn't take his eyes off him.

"I'm just like you and I'm out here on my bike," Bill went on. "That's what you'll be doing too. I don't usually fall. That was a freak thing."

Jodi took a picture of Bill and Jake. We exchanged phone numbers and I realized we'd better get going. We got back in the car. By the time we turned around, Bill was already pedaling away with his friends. And I didn't feel quite so apprehensive.

Jake came through the surgery with flying colors. The following morning, he was resting comfortably in his hospital room, dozy from painkillers. On impulse I called Bill.

"I was on my way to the hospital just now," he said. "I want to see Jake."

Minutes later Bill was there. Jake opened his eyes enough to give him a sleepy, gap-toothed smile then drifted off again.

"He looks good," Bill said. "You're probably wondering whether you made the right decision."

Jodi and I exchanged glances.

"Well, you did," Bill said. He pointed to his prosthesis. "I've been wearing this thing for about a year now. Got it after a bad infection in my foot that just wouldn't go away. Let me tell you, I was not happy at first. But you know what? My life is the same, maybe better. I'm more motivated now. That's what's going to happen with Jake. Everything he couldn't do with his bad leg before, he's going to do now."

He couldn't have known that was exactly what we needed to hear, especially me. I felt an enormous weight lift off me. "I don't know what to say, Bill, except thanks. What a lucky coincidence we met you."

Bill got a strange, almost soft look on his face. "About that," he said. "Here's the thing. I wear these cleated cycling shoes that clip into my pedals. Normally when I stop at a light, I clip out and put one foot down so I don't fall over. At that intersection yesterday my cleat got stuck in the pedal. That's why I fell and ended up on my butt when you drove up."

I glanced at Jodi again. Where was he going with this?

"Otherwise I would have zipped around the corner and been gone. I've never, ever had a problem clipping out before. And when I got back on my bike, the cleat clipped into the pedal just fine. Call it what you want, but that was no coincidence."

For a moment the hospital room was silent. I thought back to that moment at the intersection—how quiet the streets had been, how slowly I'd driven. Had I been putting off an appointment my family wasn't sure about? Or had I been led to the one appointment Someone knew we needed? A God I could always trust.

THE LAST ADDRESS
by *Sharon Harris*

Imagine a frightened teenage mom struggling on the mean streets of South Central Los Angeles. Kicked out of her home by her mother along with the rest of her siblings. She wants to believe that Momma will stop the drugs, the drinking, the dates with strange men, and take her back. Become more like the mothers on TV, the ones who care for their children, the kind of mother the girl hopes to be herself someday. At seventeen, though, she's headed down the same dead-end road.

That girl was me.

I had one boyfriend after another. Tried every drug there was. Pregnant at eleven with a son my father had custody of, then pregnant at thirteen with a daughter. I left that baby's father for Chuck, a drug dealer. He lured me with gifts and a place to stay, with him and the mother of his children. He said I would be safe with him, and convinced me that I'd found a home at last, but he controlled me the same way he controlled everybody else, with anger and threats and deadly charm. "You're not going anywhere," he told me. "No other man could possibly love you."

I lived from day to day, hand to mouth, using, being used, for close to a year. I couldn't go to my siblings, most of them haunted by the same demons that had taken our mother. I wished I could find Teddy Bear, my older sister. I'd given her that name because when we were little and shared a bed, I cuddled up to her like a teddy bear. She had married a preacher and moved to Wisconsin. Too far to get to by any bus in South Central.

All I had were my so-called friends. One night, I left my daughter with a babysitter at Chuck's and went out with my girlfriend. She was driving through an intersection when another car hit us. I managed to stagger out of the wreck, and sank to the sidewalk, dazed. I lay there, waiting for help, wondering if any would come.

A stranger appeared from nowhere, knelt beside me and took my hand. "You're going to be all right," he said. "An ambulance is on the way. God loves you and will take care of you."

"Play it up, girl," my girlfriend muttered. "If you act like you're really in pain, maybe we can get lots of money." But I didn't want money. I wanted what the man was talking about. I opened my heart and prayed, really prayed: *I'm ready, God. I want my life to be different. I don't want to be who I am anymore. Please make everything change.*

I spent the night in the emergency room, holding on to that prayer, and was released the next day. All I wanted was the love that stranger had talked about, bigger than anything Momma could give, safer than anything Chuck could offer.

I returned to Chuck's place. "I'm leaving," I told him. I packed a few things and picked up my baby to go. Chuck barred the door. The mother of his children drew a knife from the kitchen drawer and pressed it to my neck. I prayed again, thinking of that love, God's love. Chuck backed down.

"Let her go," he snarled. "She'll be back. She's got nowhere else to go."

I boarded a city bus with my baby and rode it deep into the night. *Chuck is right,* I thought. I had no home. The only place I could go was the last address I had for Momma. *I'll beg her to take us in just for the night,* I thought. *Maybe things have changed.*

It was past three in the morning when I found the place. Just like I remembered it: cracked front stoop, barred windows, peeling paint. The windows were dark and the door was bolted and locked, like all the doors of South Central at that hour.

"Momma!" I called out. No answer.

Of course. Momma never stayed in one place for very long. She wasn't waiting for me here. No one was. At 3:00 AM, nobody is going to open the door for a stranger. Especially in this neighborhood.

I sank down on the front steps, my daughter asleep in my arms. *Where to now? So much for God's love. Should I go back to Chuck?* I could still feel the knife, pressing against my throat.

Just then the door opened. A young woman in a bathrobe stepped out. "Come inside," she said.

The young woman drew a bath for me and cooked rice on the stove, with butter and a little sugar on top. "Stay as long as you like," she said. "As long as you need. Don't be afraid."

"Why would you do this for us?" I asked.

"The Lord woke me up," the woman said. "He told me, 'There is a girl with her baby outside. You must bring her in.'"

It felt like a brand-new day. We found our way to a church shelter and reached Teddy Bear by phone. She offered to help us come to Wisconsin and stay with her and her husband.

I got my GED, graduated from college, and earned a degree in counseling. Today I tell my story to the women who come to me, fleeing from abuse, emotional manipulation, the cycle of addiction and violence. I tell them that they can be free too. They can find comfort. They can find love. I should know. My life changed when a stranger opened her door, already knowing that I was there.

TWO FOR ONE

by Samuel Hooker

Back when I was pastoring a church in Portland, Oregon, I received a call early one morning from the local hospital. A patient who was dying had asked for a minister of my denomination. Could I come to the hospital as soon as possible?

Half an hour later I was standing at the bedside of Felix Richy as the nurse drew the curtain around us.

"Pastor," Mr. Richy said, "my uncle was a preacher and he used to talk to me about the Lord, but I wouldn't listen. My wife always tried to get me to go to church, but I wouldn't go. Now I'm going to meet my Maker and my life is filled with sin."

"Mr. Richy," I began, "the fact that you admit you've sinned and are willing to confess it is half the battle." We talked. I quoted some Scripture about God's forgiveness, and then we prayed together as he turned his life over to the Lord.

The next day I returned, and the next day and the next, and to the amazement of the hospital staff, Felix kept improving. In a matter of weeks he was sent home, and on the next Sunday he appeared in my church. For eight years he sat in the same pew each Sunday with hardly a miss. In the end he died suddenly of a heart attack.

I officiated at the funeral, and after the burial an elderly man approached me.

"Pastor Hooker," he said, "you don't know me, but I was in the bed next to Felix Richy when you came to the hospital that morning. I wrote down those Scriptures you quoted and gave my heart to Jesus too.

"That morning you didn't catch just one fish, you caught two. I jumped into the net while you were pulling it in."

CIRCLE OF LIFE
by Christy David

I remember the day after Easter. I had just dropped off my two-year-old daughter, Meg, at our church's preschool. My five-year-old, Will, was in the car with me. My cell phone rang just as we were about to leave. My sister Barbara calling from Savannah, her voice shaky and remote. "It's Mom. She's gone," she said. *Mom.* "And she did it to herself."

"What?" I said again and again. Suicide? Not our mother. She was a vibrant, happy person. Dad had died when my twin sisters and I were in grade school, but Mom had gone back to college the same time I went to college. She became a social worker at a hospital. A natural caregiver, full of energy and love. She was always doing something for her grandchildren, sending presents, calling, visiting, being with them. We'd just thrown her a sixtieth birthday party. The photo was still in my phone. There was Meg sitting in Mom's lap, both of them smiling.

I kept thinking maybe the autopsy would explain it. Maybe she had some horrible disease and didn't want us to know. Some deadly cancer. She'd left no note. No farewell, no explanation. Nothing. She lived with our grandmother, Nana, who had Alzheimer's. Maybe that weighed on her mind, watching her own mother sink into dementia, fearing the same would happen to her. She was always a giver, the first one to make a casserole if any friend of hers was suffering. Now it was we who were grieving.

A thousand people came to mourn her. The line spilled out the door. Everybody said what an amazing woman she was. I greeted them all, received their condolences, their hugs, but I couldn't find any relief.

Back in Atlanta I heard from the pathologist who performed the autopsy. No, there was nothing wrong. She was perfectly healthy. The best way I could explain it to Will was, "Her brain was sick and we didn't know it."

I dragged myself to the gym, to church, to be with my friends. They delivered the casseroles. I barely slept. All my clothes felt wrong, too bright and colorful, too cheerful. All I wanted was gray. One Sunday at Mass I saw a notice in the bulletin about a bereavement support group. "I need to go to that," I told my husband, Brian.

When I showed up, it was clear I'd made a mistake. Everyone in the church basement room was much older than me, widows and widowers. This wasn't the right fit. But I needed to take care of myself. I needed some support.

I started talking to a well-dressed older woman about Mom's age. We have a big congregation, and I didn't recognize her, but her last name sounded familiar from our parish prayer list. "Was your husband Bill?"

"Yes," she said. "He died after a long struggle with cancer. I took care of him all that time." So she was another caregiver, like Mom, but she seemed to have it all together. She had family nearby to look after her. A daughter who was my age.

We sat in a circle and took turns talking. Finally it was my turn. "Hello everyone, I'm Christy," I said. I tried to explain what Mom's death did to me and how alone I felt. "I don't have a mom anymore. No one to love me like she did," I said, letting the tears fall. "I guess she was under pressure at work and taking care of my grandmother. I don't think I'll ever understand it." But the part that bothered me the most was imagining her pain. "I can't get over thinking of how miserable she must have been to have committed suicide." I struggled to get my words out.

I went to the group just a few more times. Then life took over. I had to get up and take care of the family, do the shopping, the chauffeuring. A hundred times a day I'd want to pick up the phone and tell Mom something, share some little story about the children. I wondered if I would ever stop missing her. I wondered how anything good could come from such tragedy.

A year after Mom's death I got a call from an unfamiliar number. I picked up the phone hesitantly. "Christy? You might not remember me from the grief support group at church," said the caller. "I lost my husband, Bill."

"I remember," I said. I hadn't seen her since. Why was she calling now? She had moved away, she said, and joined another church. Had even met another man and fallen in love. "I've wanted to make this call for a long time. Do you have a moment?"

"Of course," I said. I quieted the children and listened.

"I wasn't sure I could bear going to the session the day you showed up," she began. "I didn't really think I could survive another moment." She described her pain, pain I knew so well. How hard it was to listen to what others were going through too. It all seemed so...hopeless. "I decided I should end my own life."

I caught my breath.

"I couldn't bear the pain anymore, the loneliness," she went on. "But meeting you changed everything. When you talked about your devastation at losing your mother, my heart broke. I just watched you cry. You were my own daughter's age and suddenly I couldn't imagine putting her through what you were going through. I could not do that to my child."

I remembered the daughter she had talked about in our church basement that day. I thought I had gone to the meeting in desperate need of help for myself. Yet there was someone there more desperate than I was. Somehow I was sent, unknowingly sent, to help her in my own pain. There was no explaining what Mom did, no understanding it, but there was this, there was some good coming from the depths of sorrow.

"You reminded me of my daughter," she said, finishing her story. "My Christy. In fact, you even have the same name."

A TALE OF TWO HOUSES
by Debra Person

This is a story of two houses. Just a few miles apart, but the distance between them couldn't have been greater. One was my downfall, the site of my spiritual abandonment. The other was my redemption, the light needed to overcome the dark places, my saving grace.

The old brownstone on Ferry Street was supposed to be a fresh start for my husband, Perc, and me. I'd just gotten out of rehab. Perc had kicked his crack habit too. We quit running hustles for money and settled down in legit jobs. We moved into the brownstone's top-floor apartment in September 1996 and were turning it into a real home—nice furniture, silk curtains, antiques Momma gave me. But addiction is a demon that doesn't relinquish its hold without a fight. All it took was one setback to send us both back to the pipe. I talked Perc into it, just like I'd turned him on to crack in the first place. "We need an escape," I said. "Just for one night."

I should've known better, known how easily one small slip spirals into full-blown relapse, considering Daddy was a heroin addict who OD'd, and I'd been in and out of rehab sixteen times. Our one night bled into days, weeks, months. Perc and I lost our jobs. Sold off our prized possessions to feed our addiction. The only thing that mattered was the next high—until I saw what rock bottom looked like one December morning in 1998.

I woke, my eyes glazed, a nasty taste in my mouth from last night's binge. Where am I? Perc snored loudly beside me. I winced. It was like I was seeing our bedroom for the first time. Stained walls. Rodent droppings. No furniture except our filthy mattress, the floor around it littered with soda cans and tire gauges we'd used for pipes. The place looked the way I felt. Seedy. Debased. Stripped bare.

If I stay here, I'm going to die, I thought. Panic rose, mutated into hysteria. "I can't live like this anymore!" I cried, shaking Perc awake. "You've got to get me out of here!"

Even lost in his own addiction, this man would do anything for me. Perc remembered a place he'd passed once. Serenity House, a shelter for women. He called them up for me. They had one bed left.

And one condition—no drug use allowed.

I went there that same day. The house was beautiful, a well-kept two-story. I raised my hand to knock on the door. A brightness came from inside, warm and welcoming. Still I hesitated. Was I ready to leave Perc? Could I kick my habit? I'd failed sixteen times. Why would this time be any different?

The door opened. Before I could take a step, a force tugged me over the threshold, gentle yet irresistible. A voice—one that I sensed rather than heard out loud—said, *This is where you're supposed to be.*

And it was. For the first time, I really listened to my counselors and to the other women rebuilding their lives. I talked too—about how I'd been molested as a child and raped as a teenager, how surviving made me hard on the outside but left me hollow inside, how I turned to drugs to fill, or at least escape, that void. They heard it all, and they didn't judge me. They loved me, and they told me that God loved me even more. I wanted to believe it, wanted to believe that His was the voice I'd heard.

But after two months of living drug-free, I felt the stirrings of an old craving. For Perc. He loved me too, enough to let me go. I had to see him, hold him, ease my guilt for getting him hooked on crack. I went back to the place we'd tried so hard to turn into a home, the old brownstone on Ferry Street.

I climbed the stairs. The door to the apartment was hanging off its hinges. "Perc?"

He wasn't home. Disappointed, I wandered from room to room. Eyed the empty spaces, the bare closets. In the corner, I spotted the old toothbrush I'd used to clean a pair of shoes I sold for a hit. Perc's leather couch, the antique turntable Momma had given me, the silk drapery, dishes and silverware—all of it gone.

I scanned the bedroom. Makeshift pipes—broken glass tubes that used to hold fake roses—were scattered on the floor. I scooped up one, soiled by residue from a previous smoke, and ran my fingers along the length of it.

There were footsteps on the stairs. Perc.

I peered around the bedroom door, saw him go into the kitchen. Just as I was about to call out to him, he pulled a rock from his pocket. Then came the familiar click of a lighter, the suck of breath against a wire filter, a piece of steel wool. I stood frozen, watching Perc inhale what made us believe we could fly straight to the moon together. My wanting for it wet my mouth.

My throat and lungs seized up, the demon of addiction suffocating me. I closed my eyes, tilted my head back. *Call out to Perc. Tell him you're here.*

"Help me, God," escaped from my lips instead.

Slowly I opened my eyes. I couldn't see the kitchen anymore. Or Perc. Darkness shrouded me, as if I'd entered a tunnel. The pitch black blinded me to everything but the light at the end. The front door, hanging open. I felt that same irresistible force that tugged me over the threshold of Serenity House, only this time with more intensity. It carried me out the door, down the stairs, out of the brownstone, like some kind of divine gravity. When my feet finally touched the ground, I was standing on the corner. I looked back, hoping to see Perc.

He wasn't there.

Someone else was, though. The only force more powerful than my addiction, the only love greater than the one I was leaving behind. Someone I could release my guilt to, and put my trust in completely. That day I walked away from my past and through the doors of Serenity House again, toward the light of my future.

THE LOST SISTER
by Theresa Crowder

For years I'd wondered about her, my little sister. What was her name? What was she like? Was she happy? Did she even know she'd been given up for adoption, and did she ever wonder about us? My older brother, Richard, and I talked about how she could be somebody we passed in the street without realizing it...or perhaps she was living with a well-to-do family thousands of miles away. I worried—if we ever found her, would she like us? Maybe if she knew about us she would be grateful she wasn't raised in the dysfunctional home that Richard and I grew up in.

I was seventeen when Mom told me about her. Mom married when she was fifteen. She dropped out of high school and Dad worked in a steel mill. They got a small place in Chicago and had Richard, then me a year later. The truth is, my parents were very young and my dad made bad decisions. One was to rob a gas station with a buddy of his. I was just a toddler when he was sentenced to a year in prison. My mom was encouraged by her family to file for divorce even though she was still very much in love with my dad. After he was released they were divorced but would still see each other in secret to avoid disapproval from the family. When my mom discovered she was pregnant, she knew she wouldn't be able to give the new baby a good life. She could hardly manage raising two kids as it was, and her secret relationship with my dad had come to an end. Giving the baby up was the hardest choice she'd ever made. As soon as Mom told me about my sister, I wanted to find her. Illinois law at the time, however, made it impossible.

Richard and I always shared a special bond. We were inseparable. Mom remarried when we were still young. We welcomed several half siblings, and to Mom's credit, she did the best she could to provide us with a good home. My senior year of high school I met Richard's best friend Randy. We fell in love, got married, and settled in Arkansas. I worked as a mail carrier and we gave our kids the kind of stable home I'd longed for as a child.

But Richard? He struggled. In high school he clashed with our stepfather and got into drinking and drugs. He married young and had a son, but his wife left him. After that, he drifted. He ended up homeless in Florida. I worried constantly about my big brother. He called once a month to tell me he was okay, though he wasn't and I knew it. Finally I couldn't stand it anymore. I sent him a bus ticket and persuaded him to come to Arkansas and live with me. I didn't care how messed up he was. He needed help and I knew I was the only one who could give it to him.

Richard moved in and found a job as a painter. Eventually, he got a place of his own a few blocks from ours. He still had problems, but he was softhearted and so caring to those he loved most—his family. Our kids were crazy about him—even their friends called him Uncle Rich. Randy had been diagnosed with diabetes, and Richard would always help take care of him while I was at work.

We started talking again about finding our little sister. We needed more information from Mom. She remembered the name of the adoption agency, but they couldn't, by law, release any details. All the state of Illinois could do was give us forms to fill out, so if our sister contacted the department of records, she could find out her birth family's medical history.

Before we could file those forms, Mom needed to sign them. But something always got in the way. She was in bad health, so I was planning a trip to Chicago to take care of it myself, but then Richard was diagnosed with lymphoma. I watched my brother's health deteriorate quickly over the next few months. I prayed for a miracle, that God would help him beat this disease. It wasn't to be. He died four months later.

The short obituary the funeral home posted online listed surviving relatives, mostly half siblings from Mom's and Dad's second marriages. I'd lost the one person who understood how painful our childhood had been, the only other person who understood what finding our sister meant to me. I was devastated; I asked God, *Why was he taken from us so soon?*

I was still reeling from Richard's death a month later, when I got a phone call from Mom. "Theresa, I don't know how to tell you this. Guess who just called me? Your sister!"

I almost dropped the phone.

"Her name's Jodi," Mom went on in a rush. "She's married, has kids, and lives in Chicago! She wants to talk to you. Here's her number."

With Randy at my side, I dialed the number, my fingers trembling. A warm voice answered. "This is Jodi."

"Hello, Jodi," I began, trying to control my emotions. "It's...your sister. Theresa."

"Theresa!" Suddenly we were both talking at once. Jodi had always known she was adopted, and often wondered about her birth family. As it turned out, she'd grown up in the same suburbs of south Chicago as Richard and me. Two of her three children graduated from the same high school I had graduated from. Her husband worked at the same cement company where my stepfather had worked years earlier. Now she lived five minutes away from a cousin I visited every summer.

How many times had we just missed each other over the years? I thought, my heart breaking a little more that Richard had died too soon. *He should have been part of this.*

Jodi explained that the law had recently changed in Illinois and she was finally able to get a copy of her original birth certificate. Mom's name was on it. "I searched for her online, but because she'd remarried and has a different last name now, I couldn't find anything. Except for one obituary for a man with the last name I'd been born with. Richard's obituary."

Jodi must have thought I'd hung up. I couldn't say a word. "I wish I could have met him," Jodi said. "What was he like?"

What was Richard like? Hurt, troubled, seeking to heal his pain—often in all the wrong ways. But he was also a devoted older brother, a caring brother-in-law, a loving uncle. Someone who'd been on a journey to healing these past several years. A journey that didn't end with his death. He'd brought me and our sister together, made our family whole. One last act of brotherly love.

THE FENCE JOB
by Phil Wilder

"Hi, Phil? It's Carolyn. Listen, my father desperately needs someone to help him with a fence he's building at the ranch. He's seventy-six and, well, he needs to get it finished before the ground gets too dry and hard. Would you have a few days to help out as a ranch hand?"

I replayed her words in my mind long after I hung up the phone. For weeks I'd been hoping against hope for the right opportunity to open up, a match for my skills. But this unexpected favor for a friend wasn't the answer.

I needed a job. A real job. A reason to get up in the morning. I was still reeling from being laid off, my position as business manager at a construction firm eliminated, just like that. It was the economy, my boss said. But it felt like something more. As though I'd hit a dead end.

At age thirty-six, my life was unraveling. Even my marriage of fourteen years was over. Irreconcilable differences. Where was I supposed to go from here? What was I even good at? Not at being a husband, apparently, and that really hurt. Business? I knew how to bid on a building project. How to order supplies. How to build a house from the ground up. Once, years ago, I'd worked as an EMT. But where had any of that gotten me? I combed through the want ads every day, but no one seemed to be looking for someone with my particular skills. It was as if I didn't fit into the world anymore. It had been days since I'd even left the house. I'd prayed for guidance, for direction, but apparently I wasn't much good at that either.

I thought about Carolyn's call again. She had told me that the ranch was up in the Sierra Nevada foothills. It'd be beautiful in May. I didn't know the first thing about stringing barbed wire, but I could follow directions. Some fresh air couldn't hurt. Might even do me good.

Reluctantly I called Carolyn back and told her I would do it. The next day I was driving down a dusty dirt road to her family's ranch, twenty long miles from the nearest town.

Carolyn, her father, Clyde Werly, and his wife, Jean, came out to greet me. The ranch house was beautiful, rustic, and homey, with an orange orchard and fields of wildflowers around it. Clyde shook my hand, his grip firm. He wore boots and a cowboy hat. His thick white hair and the lines of his face were the only clues to his age.

"I'm glad you could make it," he said, his eyes sizing me up. "These days I'm moving a little slower than I used to. And we're working against time. The clay in the soil here can get like concrete come summer. But we'll get 'er done."

Over a dinner of roast beef, baked potatoes, and green beans, Clyde told me that he had spent his life in the mountains. His parents had built the ranch in the early part of the twentieth century. And Clyde himself had worked for years in fire control with the Forest Service. He was a man's man.

"Dad taught my sister and me how to fly-fish before we could read," Carolyn said with a laugh. I'd forgotten how pretty she was, with long, dark blonde hair and blue eyes. And she even fly-fished.

"We'll get at it tomorrow at seven AM," Clyde said, standing and stretching when dinner was over. "Gotta get going before the sun gets too hot."

In the morning we loaded his pickup with a posthole digger, fence posts, barbed wire, and a cooler of water, and set out for the site of the new fence.

Clyde showed me how to work the posthole digger, slamming its double blades into the ground over and over, but still hardly making a dent. Sweat had begun streaming down his face.

"Here, I can do that," I offered. "Once I get the posts in you can string the wire."

The clay was no more pliable for me, no matter how hard I hammered it with the digger. Soon my muscles were on fire. But I kept at it, until finally a hole emerged deep enough for the first post. I moved down a few yards. *Wham!*

By late morning the sun was beating down on us. I was exhausted, my throat as dry as sandpaper. It had taken four hours to dig maybe a dozen holes. Pitiful! I looked back toward the truck—and the water cooler. I needed a drink. I could just make out Clyde, nearly a hundred yards away.

I hiked back to him. Clyde was sitting under a tree, his shirt soaked through with perspiration.

"Let's take a break," I said. "I'll get us some water." I walked to the truck and filled two bottles. Then I turned back. Clyde started to stand, but only made it to his knees before collapsing to the ground.

Heart attack!

I raced to Clyde and rolled his limp body face-up. His eyes stared at me blankly. I felt for a pulse. Nothing. I reached for his mouth, but his jaw was clenched tight, like a vise. "Clyde," I shouted, "I've got to get you breathing!" I thought back to my EMT training, but my mind was blank. My hands trembled. CPR. Clyde needed it. Now.

I grabbed his jaw more firmly, opening his mouth slightly. I pinched his nose and placed my lips over his. I blew out my breath, trying to force air into his body. Then again. I pushed down hard at the center of his chest with both hands. Released, then pushed down again. Thirty times. Just as I'd been taught. It all came back to me. Two breaths. Thirty more compressions.

Still no sign of life.

"Clyde, come back!" I cried. "God, don't let him die. Please help me." Two breaths. Pump. Thirty times. I needed to get him to a hospital. But it was impossible to drive and give CPR at the same time. The nearest hospital was probably at least an hour away. No way to call for help. I was his only hope. I had to breathe. Pump. And pray.

For as long as it took.

It was no use. He was completely unresponsive. I dropped my hands from his chest and sagged back on my heels. Defeated. Who was I to think I could beat death? I felt a sob well up from deep in my chest. I started to cover my face. I looked into Clyde's eyes one last time.

He blinked.

He blinked! "Can you hear me?" I cried. "*Clyde!* Can you hear me?"

"What happened?" Clyde said, his voice a whisper. "Did I pass out?"

"Yes," I said, fighting to sound calm. "Let's rest for a minute. Then we need to get you to a doctor."

"A doctor?" Clyde said. "No, I'll be fine. Just let me sit for a bit. Then we'll get back at it."

"You weren't breathing," I said. "I had to give you CPR. I think you might have had a heart attack!"

"Okay," he said, "I'll see a doctor, if it will make you feel better."

At the ER I told the doctor everything that had happened. He rushed Clyde off for an electrocardiogram and an echocardiogram, then a stress test. I sat with Carolyn and her mother in the waiting room, praying. I worried that I'd taken too long to get his heart beating. There could be brain damage. Neurological problems.

The doctor returned looking oddly cheerful. "Our brains are constantly signaling our hearts to beat," he said to Carolyn. "It happens automatically. But very rarely the signal doesn't get through. That's what seems to have happened to your father. Technically, he was dead."

This was good news? Really? I didn't understand.

The doctor looked at me. "He's alive because you were able to quickly get his heart beating again. Another minute and it would have been too late. You saved his life. We want to keep him overnight just to be sure, but there's no sign of any permanent damage. His heart is completely healthy."

Carolyn grabbed my hand, then threw her arms around me. "I don't know how to thank you," she said.

I was still processing the doctor's words. Everything that had happened—I knew it wasn't only me who had come to Clyde's aid. What was the chance of me going back for water at that exact moment? Or of me—a guy suddenly with nothing but time on his hands and just enough CPR training—being at the ranch in the first place? Maybe I wasn't where I wanted to be, but I was where I needed to be.

It turned out that Clyde wasn't the only reason for me being there. Two years later Carolyn and I were married. And I started a new career, doing leadership training for businesses. I don't worry anymore about where my life is headed. I just look forward to finding out where I'll be led next.

RECOVERED
by Kallee Krong-McCreery

It was them. I was sure. I caught my breath.

My husband and I were out to dinner, and when I looked up from my menu I saw them, intensely familiar and yet different. They were older now, the strain of years showing, but those faces had burned themselves into my memory. "That's them," I said. "The happy couple."

My husband looked at me, nonplussed. For about half a year I'd stared at pieces of this couple's life, photos in an old album. We'd found it in the gutter on a street by our house. A handsome young man at his high school graduation. A dark-haired, exotic beauty winking at the camera. Their backyard wedding. Babies growing into toddlers, playing with grandparents. It was the story of a happy family. No one could have meant to throw away these precious moments.

If only I could find these people, I thought. And yet where to start? I had no idea. So I kept the album, thumbed through it from time to time, wondering.

Now, improbably, here they were. There was something so different about them, though. As if they were strangers to each other. They picked at their food. I couldn't contain myself. I shot up from my seat and approached them. "I have something that belongs to you," I said.

Immediately, I felt like I was intruding. Yes, they said, they'd lost the album, among other items looted from a storage locker. Storage locker? Maybe these photos hadn't been missed. I jotted down my address, unsure if they even wanted the album returned.

The next day, the man showed up at our house. "We were caught off guard," he explained apologetically. Then he took the album from me and flipped through it, smiling wistfully.

"You see, this was back when I was sober. Before my drug addiction destroyed our marriage. I'm getting my life together, and hoped my wife and I could be a family again. If we could remember what connected us. That dinner last night was the first step," he said.

He held the album to his chest. "Then you ran up, offering us this."

Maybe, I hoped, because it was meant to be the next step.

CHAPTER 7

In the Hands of God

A CALL FOR HELP
by Julia Eie

"Help! Please, somebody, help!"

I looked out the window at the orchard, dark and shadowy in the pale moonlight. It was a woman's voice. Close. But where? My son was at a friend's house. It couldn't be him watching a scary show on TV.

I lived in Milton-Freewater, Oregon, at the time, renting a garage apartment set back from our landlord's house. The orchard and a small creek were behind us, not much else. Maybe someone fell in the water. Or was lost.

"Somebody, please help me!" There it was again! A woman, desperate and very near. I grabbed the phone and called the police. "I think a woman is being attacked," I told the dispatcher. I gave my address. "Please hurry!"

I waited. The shouts continued. I called the police again. "We sent an officer already," the dispatcher said. "He didn't find anything unusual. But I can send him back, I suppose."

Had I imagined the voice? No. There it was again. *The police should have found her by now.* I called one more time. "Where are you?" I asked.

This time the dispatcher put me through to an officer. "Ma'am," he said, cutting me off, "we went out there. There were no screams. No sign of anything. Stop calling, or we'll file a complaint against you."

I hung up. I *knew* I wasn't hearing things. *I need to look myself,* I thought. I got in my car and drove to the orchard, my window rolled down. Every time I thought I was close, the shouts got further away. I passed the orchard and drove on. A quarter mile. Half a mile. A mile. Then I saw a faint glow ahead. I drove toward it. There, on a barren stretch of road, was a car, wedged into a steep ditch. Standing next to it was a teenage girl, crying. "My boyfriend is stuck inside," she said. "Please help us."

I called the police and told them exactly where to go. Within minutes, two squad cars and an ambulance arrived.

"I told you I heard someone shouting," I said to one of the officers.

"So you're the one," the officer said. "Do you see where we are, lady? There's no way you could have heard her from inside your house. We're almost three miles away."

A GLOW IN THE NIGHT

by Stuart Reininger

Something about the sea can drive men mad. How else to explain all those stories of alluring mermaids, terrifying sea monsters, and ghost ships? Like the legend of the *Flying Dutchman,* forever floating above the waves, its long-dead crew delivering dire warnings to the spooked sailors of passing vessels. As a writer and sailor, I find these stories fascinating, but the name of my thirty-five-foot sailboat reflects how I feel about them—*Tall Tales.*

My buddy Tristan was like me, which is why I thought he was pulling my leg when he revealed his own unlikely tale. He had been on a long solo voyage in his small sailboat, and was sleeping belowdecks with the boat on autopilot. Something awakened him in his bunk, and thinking he'd hit rough seas, he ran up on deck. "I swear to you," Tristan told me, "at the helm was a guy dressed like a seventeenth-century sailor."

"Come on." I rolled my eyes.

"The guy yelled at me," Tristan insisted, "in Spanish: 'I can't do everything...you have to do the rest.'" The mysterious sailor gestured ahead. A supertanker was bearing down on Tristan's boat.

Tristan pushed the man aside and grabbed the tiller, turning the boat hard to starboard, narrowly avoiding a collision. The tanker's bow wave heaved his boat over, and when it righted itself, the upper spreader and the boom were seriously damaged. "I was lucky to be alive," Tristan said. "The tanker crew never even saw me."

"And the seventeenth-century Spanish dude?" I asked.

"Gone." Of course he was.

I thought about Tristan's story while I got *Tall Tales* ready for my annual winter migration from New York City to Florida. Ted, the marina's dockmaster, warned me that a nor'easter was churning toward the coast. I wasn't worried. My first stop was Manasquan, New Jersey, only forty miles south. The predicted storm wouldn't arrive until late that night—long after I would be safely tucked in. I'd spend a few days visiting friends and wait for a weather window for my next jump offshore.

Tall Tales tugged at her lines as the first eddies of the ebb rippled the water. That tide would become a torrent flushing us down the East River, through New York Harbor, under the Verrazano-Narrows Bridge and out to sea. "You sure you're comfortable with this, Stu?" Ted asked again.

"Sure. I'll be in with time to spare. I'll see you in the spring." I gave a cheerful wave as I cast off.

New York was far astern when *Tall Tales* lifted to a steep sea, slid into a trough, then accelerated upward, climbing yet another white-capped wave. The seas were choppy but the wind was aft and that meant I'd arrive ahead of schedule. Sure enough, shortly after noon I spotted Manasquan's sea buoy and began angling in toward shore. The waves had become steep, sharp ridges, tops blown into spume by a howling wind. Dark clouds hung overhead. The storm had outrun the forecaster's prediction. I breathed a sigh of relief. *Thank God I made it here in time.*

A wave rocked the boat. I steadied myself and looked ahead. Instead of welcoming jetties lining a calm inlet, a column of roiling breakers smashed into the seawalls. The inlet's entrance churned and spun like a washing machine. No way could I get in.

The sea morphed into a maelstrom—spray, crashing waves, the screams of a full-fledged gale. I had no choice. Forget Manasquan and run south, ahead of the storm—the only direction possible—to find safe harbor. Just as I changed my heading, *Tall Tales* slammed into a trough. My electronics flickered out. No radar, no GPS, no running lights. *Tall Tales* was tossed about in the gathering darkness by the rage of a full-blown nor'easter.

I hoped to reach the Atlantic City Inlet, fifty miles—some ten hours—south, but without instrumentation, an entrance would be impossible. If I turned shoreward at the wrong point, waves would smash me into the Brigantine shoals, a line of reefs far off the Jersey shore that for centuries has snared unwary ships. I needed to hang on, steer downwind—and stay alert. I couldn't let the boat broach and sink. If the storm didn't blow itself out, I'd eventually be propelled onto the reefs surrounding Cape Hatteras, known as the graveyard of the Atlantic.

Night fell. The last light drained from the sky. Grimly I hung on to the wheel, fighting to keep my course in the dark. By midnight, I'd been sixteen hours at the helm and the storm showed no signs of abating. *Tall Tales* catapulted over another wave. The flash of a red beacon pierced the night. The buoy marking the Brigantine shoals. *Those accursed shoals.* I edged *Tall Tales* further offshore, just seaward of the reef line. But I was losing it.

I would drift off to sleep, then snap awake as the boat slipped off course. Silently praying, I tried to stay awake. If I could just hang on till dawn. The light would help me navigate.

Something was ahead of me. A massive hulk, a darker gray than the surrounding gloom. Another ship? It was there and then it wasn't. Like a ghostly vision. I rubbed my eyes. There! The glow of a green light appeared out of the mist. Then...nothing. If it was a ship and that was his starboard running light, then he was crossing my course, heading west. How could he be going west? He would crash into the shoals. Unless he was going into the Delaware ship channel off Delaware Bay. Was I that far south? I had no idea.

That can't be a ship, I thought. *No one else would be out in this.* I was so tired, I was hallucinating. Reason said I should keep heading south. But something more powerful, more persuasive than reason grabbed me. I gave in to a strange, outlandish impulse. I twisted the wheel to starboard. *Tall Tales* careened onto her new course—westward. I was going to follow that light, hallucination or not.

I kept expecting the sickening *crunch* of a vessel running aground. Instead, the wind and seas began to subside. I had no sense of time, space; all was blackness and rain, driving sheets of rain. I blinked hard to clear it out of my eyes. I was in protected water! Land to the north and south. Delaware Bay.

I slowly steered north, into shallower waters. In a trance, I kicked the anchor overboard. The chain rattled out, then stopped. I went below, collapsed onto my bunk, and fell into a deep, dreamless sleep.

"Hello? Hey, anybody aboard?"

I opened my eyes. Sunlight slatted through the cabin. Dazed, I staggered on deck into a beautiful, calm day.

A fisherman in a small skiff was alongside. "Is there a problem? Why are you anchored here?"

"I'm okay. A bit tired. I came in late last night and just dropped the hook."

"You came in last night? In that gale? No way."

I nodded. "I lucked out. I'd still be out there—or on the bottom—if I hadn't followed a ship in." I recounted my adventure.

The fisherman shook his head. "That can't be right. The Coasties closed the channel yesterday. A tug lost his tow and there's a half-dozen barges floating around out there. No ship could come in or out. Don't know how you managed to."

I looked around. The fisherman was right. Barges blocked the channel. No ship looked like the one I'd followed in. "But I saw his light, and took the same course, found my way in," I insisted.

The fisherman rolled his eyes. "Of course you did."

FOOD FOR A CAUSE

by Carol Ermo

Brr. I hugged the warm Crock-Pot I was carrying as I walked up to the building site. We're hardy folk here in Wisconsin, but that fall day was beyond brisk. The women in my church group were bringing lunch to some Habitat for Humanity volunteers building a house in a working-class neighborhood. We'd made brownies, sandwiches and, most important, a huge batch of chili. Nearing the site, I wondered if chili would be enough to warm the bellies of the hungry crew.

Except...there was no activity. No hammering. No saws buzzing. No drills whirring. No one working inside or out. Only one car was parked on the street. A man climbed out, pulling his jacket tight. "Didn't anyone tell you ladies?" he said. "There's no build today."

"No build? Why?" I asked.

"Windows didn't come in," the man explained. "There's not much to do without them. It's so cold, we figured we'd hold off until they're delivered."

The pot of chili felt heavy. All that work we'd put in, chopping onions, browning the beef, mixing in the spices and waiting for it to cook. Now we had this enormous batch and no one to eat it. Maybe we'd split it up. My family would have supper for weeks. Then a thought popped into my head that didn't seem to come from me. *Take it to the homeless shelter.*

The shelter? They planned way ahead and I was sure they already had a meal for the day. Then again, they could freeze the chili and serve it some other time. The women and I piled back into the car and drove to the shelter.

A crowd of people huddled outside the cafeteria doors.

"What's going on?" I asked the shelter coordinator.

"The group that was supposed to fix the meal today didn't come in," she said. "We've got all these people and nothing to feed them."

"You have something now," I said.

There was enough chili for everyone...even for two stragglers who arrived after I thought the pot was empty. I shouldn't have been surprised. This crew wasn't the one we'd been planning to serve, but the Master Builder obviously had a greater plan.

THE CASE OF THE BAIL JUMPER

by Aaron Horsley

I don't normally talk about my job. As a bail-bond agent, with the cases I'm involved in, it's best to keep a low profile. I've got to assume that the people I track down, the ones running away from the law, are dangerous. But it wasn't until a recent case that I realized I might not always be the one in danger.

Late one Wednesday, I pulled a file from the stack of about a dozen manila folders on my desk. A straightforward drunk-driving case. Let's call the guy J.D. Class C misdemeanor, just over the legal limit. My company posted bail, five thousand dollars, but J.D. was a no-show for his date with the judge. Now there was a warrant out on him.

Easy enough, I thought. J.D. owned a business. We had his work address, home address, vehicle description, and booking photo on file. I waited till 10:00 PM—I do my best investigative work after dark—then left to stake out his store.

I pulled my car into the strip mall and idled in the shadows. The store lights were off; the company's sign had disappeared. His vehicle, a large SUV, was nowhere in sight.

Probably holed up at home, I thought. I drove over to J.D.'s apartment complex. There was that SUV, in a parking spot. Still had the magnetic labels with his business's name and everything. Gotcha, I thought.

You've got to be careful bringing in a bail jumper. That *Dog the Bounty Hunter* show isn't really how it's done. If you go storming in, the guy might bolt, or react violently. So I called the super of the complex and explained who I was. He agreed to knock on the door and confirm that J.D. was at home. Meanwhile, I kept my eye trained on that SUV. If J.D. ran for it, I'd stop him.

The super returned, shaking his head. "I keyed into the apartment. He's not there." *Tomorrow's another day*, I thought, and called it a night.

Thursday evening, though, same story. That SUV hadn't budged. *Maybe he's left the state*, I thought. I'd seen it before—a guy will do almost anything to avoid jail.

Just then, a smaller SUV zoomed past me, out of the apartment complex. I only caught a glimpse of the driver…but he had the same build, same hair color as the guy in the booking photo. I remained at my post in case I was wrong—besides, I didn't want to get into a car chase. But I had a hunch it was my guy. I was getting closer.

Friday, I got up early and made some calls. I found an interesting piece of news. J.D. had moved his place of business. Not too far away.

I pulled into the lot and saw his sign. That same small SUV too, the one I'd seen the night before. This was it. My chance to nab him. I geared up—bulletproof vest, Taser, bail-enforcement badge—and approached the store.

I opened the door. "Freeze!" I said, flashing my badge. "I have a warrant for your arrest."

J.D. sat at his desk in the rear of the store, typing away at his computer. The place was empty except for us. He looked up. Froze.

"You're under arrest," I repeated. "Get down on the ground."

J.D. jumped up and ran into the back room. Remember what I said about people who run away from the law being dangerous? I gripped my Taser, which can deliver an incapacitating but not fatal jolt of electricity, and sidestepped my way toward the back room. I peered around the corner and scoped out the situation.

J.D. was hiding behind a pallet, not very successfully.

This time I shouted. "Get down on the ground, sir, or I'll use force!"

"I won't," J.D. said. He stepped out from behind the pallet. He had tears in his eyes. "Just shoot me, man," he said, staring straight at me. "I don't want to live anymore. Do it. Shoot me!"

Is this guy serious? He must have thought I was holding a gun, not a Taser. He was trying to commit what we call suicide by cop. I aimed the red target beam at his chest. "Let me handcuff you. Or else I'll have to stun you, then cuff you. First option will hurt a whole lot less."

He stayed still, silent, staring at me, tears spilling down his cheeks. Finally, he crouched on the ground and held up his hands. I took hold of him and snapped the cuffs around his wrists. *Case closed,* I thought. *Next stop, jail.*

I surveyed the empty store. The windows were open. The computer on. I didn't want to leave things unsecured. As J.D. crouched on the floor, I closed the windows, then went to shut down the computer.

A document was up on the computer screen. An e-mail, half-written. I checked it out, scrolled down. "Difficulties..." "Living a repetitive life..." "Can't take it anymore..." My blood ran cold. It was a suicide note.

"My wife's left me," J.D. said, sobbing. "She fled the country and took our daughter with her. I have nothing left. And now this...."

I looked into his bloodshot eyes. His words echoed in my ears: *Just shoot me.* The truth dawned on me. What if I'd arrived a moment later? What was he planning to do to himself? I knelt on the ground beside him. I felt I owed him more than just bringing him in. He was a fellow human being in terrible pain.

"God," I prayed, "please bless this man. Open up his heart so that he can let You in again." We knelt together for a long moment.

"Is that the reason you didn't show up for your court dates?" I finally asked him. "You've given up?"

J.D. seemed confused. "What court dates?" he asked. "My attorney never said a word about it."

I looked him in the eye. I've heard every excuse in the book, but something about this man told me he wasn't lying.

"You're not going to run, are you?" He shook his head. I let him out of his handcuffs, something I'd never done before in my career. He was no bail jumper. I was legally obligated to bring him in, and he would have to wait until Monday for another hearing. But this man wasn't a threat to anybody but himself.

Come Monday, J.D. pleaded his case in court. I stood beside him and told the judge my company was willing to stay the bond. Promised he'd show up for his next date.

And he did. J.D. complied with the law for the remainder of his case, followed the court's orders, and got his record clean. I'm still in touch with him. He's doing much better now. He gets to see his daughter. He's thankful to be around.

I'm thankful too. I called J.D.'s attorneys after I brought him in—I don't leave stones unturned—and asked about the court dates J.D. had missed. J.D.'s story checked out: His case had slipped through the cracks, the secretary admitted. They'd never notified him.

Instead, the court notified me. And that's why I was on his case, just in time.

ONE LAST ONION

by Lois Kennedy

Huckleberry Hound's lazy drawl drifted into my kitchen that Saturday morning in the fall of 1959. His antics would keep my two young children occupied while I cooked some oatmeal for breakfast. The television was a poor babysitter, but what other option did I have? My husband had left us. We got no support from him, financial or otherwise. We'd lost everything we owned in a fire and had to start over from scratch. There wasn't much assistance for single mothers back then, so the free entertainment the television offered was a big help.

I opened the cupboard to see what I could make for dinner later. Not much. Some nights I felt like I was trying to conjure a meal out of nothing. I cooked little more than beans, spaghetti, macaroni, and tuna casserole. "Looks like beans again," I said, taking the lone bag off the shelf. We enjoyed them as long as something gave them flavor: beans with ham hock, beans with ground beef. Tonight, though, all I had was a single onion.

One onion. How had it come to this? We were surviving, but barely. I was angry with God. I couldn't help it. *Can't You see we're struggling, Lord? Can't You show us You care?*

I had just finished washing the oatmeal pot when there was a knock at the door. It was Theresa from across the street. We weren't the only family in the neighborhood scraping by. Theresa and her husband were too, with four little girls to raise. Even so, on weekdays, she'd take my son to school with her kids and watch him in the afternoons until I got home from my job as a switchboard operator. I didn't know what I'd do without her.

"Could I borrow an onion?" Theresa asked. "I'm making beans for dinner and I've run out."

I can't spare it, I thought. I could say I was out as well. But I didn't. She'd done so much for me.

"Sure, Theresa, I just happen to have one," I said.

As I reached into the cupboard, a Bible verse came to mind: "Whatsoever you shall give in My name, it shall be returned to you one hundredfold." Ha. When did I ever get a hundredfold anything? *Okay, God,* I thought, handing over my last onion, *I'm giving in Your name. Let's see if You're true to Your Word.* It wasn't a prayer, it was a frustrated challenge.

No onions appeared in the laundry room or tumbled out of the cupboards after Theresa left. I went to the living room to do some cleaning. Another knock at the door. Theresa again? No. A Watkins salesman was standing there. Watkins men were a familiar sight, going door to door selling household items, spices, and other things I couldn't afford. "You're wasting your time here," I told the man. "I'm sorry, but I just can't buy anything."

He looked around my sparse living room. "I understand," he said. "You have a nice day, ma'am." He turned to leave, then stopped, reaching into his bag. "Here, try this," he said. He held out a small envelope.

I pushed it right back. "I really can't afford anything," I said firmly.

"It's a free sample," he said. "We just want to see if people like it."

"Well, if there's no charge.... You have a nice day too."

The Watkins man walked down the block. I held up the envelope to read the label.

I didn't know it, but better times were ahead. Soon I'd meet a man who would become my husband for the next fifty years. My kids would go on to have families of their own. We'd be well cared for. All I knew right then was that we'd enjoy our beans that night. Flavored with hundreds of dehydrated onion flakes. Compliments of the Watkins man.

THE HOUSE AT THE END OF THE ROAD
by Judy Couch

Our school bus skidded, the tires losing their grip on the slippery river road. My heart raced. All I could think was, *I'm too young to die!*

I clutched the edge of my seat. The narrow road wound along a steep slope, dicey even under normal conditions, but this morning it was coated with a slick layer of ice. I could see the river below—a thirty-foot drop. I pictured the bus somersaulting into its freezing waters, the headlines in tomorrow's paper. *Michigan Teen Dies in Icy Plunge—Never Even Made It to Prom.* My devastated parents. Our whole community in mourning.

If it weren't for one tiny house at the end of this dead-end road, we wouldn't even be in this mess. But the boy who lived there had just been added to our bus route. No wonder the county hadn't plowed or salted here. There were hardly any other houses up this way. Who would ever want to live out in the middle of nowhere?

The school bus fishtailed down the road and we picked up the kid. I tried not to glare at him. No one made a sound until we finally reached the turn onto the highway, the plowed, ice-free highway. I exhaled. Everybody started talking again, about the school dance, the football game, home-work, pop quizzes. We were safe—for now.

But what about the ride back?

I tried to concentrate in my classes that morning, but my stomach churned every time I thought about the river road. What good would algebra do me now? Something bad was going to happen that afternoon. I just knew it.

At lunch I stopped by the main office to pick up a book from the school secretary. Someone was talking quietly in the principal's office. I lingered outside, biting my nails.

"It's too dangerous," a gruff voice said. I recognized that voice. Mr. Adams, the bus driver.

"Are you sure?" the principal asked.

"This morning we came close to going in the river," Mr. Adams said. "I don't know what we're gonna do."

I bolted out of the office and collapsed against the lockers, shaking. Even Mr. Adams was freaked. Why couldn't the boy's parents just come and pick him up?

The afternoon bell rang. We all got on the bus. I sank down low in my seat. I didn't want to talk with my friends. The sun was shining, but it was still freezing cold. When we reached the exit onto the river road, all I could see was sparkling ice. Mr. Adams wiped the sweat on his forehead with the back of his hand. He was about to turn. *Please, dear God, save us!*

This was it. We were going to skid over the edge. I squeezed my eyes shut, waiting for something. Glass shattering. Screaming. All I heard, though, was a low rumble. We weren't moving. I opened my eyes.

A huge truck had pulled in front of us. Sand and gravel spilled from its load bed onto the treacherous road, covering the ice. It churned ahead, maneuvering the turns with ease.

Mr. Adams turned and followed the trail the truck had left, all the way to the house at the end of the road. The boy jumped off the bus and ran inside. Mr. Adams, though, didn't turn around right away. He just sat there, scratching his head. What was he waiting for?

Then I looked to see what Mr. Adams was so confused about. The gravel trail ended right in front of the tiny house, but the gravel truck— where had it gone?

BLOWOUT

by Virginia Topham

The reddish cloud of dust billowing up from our pickup tires blurred my view of pines, juniper, and sage. These were drought conditions, drier even than usual for the first week of August in southern Oregon. We were careful whenever we came out to our summer pasture, sixteen miles from pavement and thirty-five miles from our home ranch. To get to this irrigated meadowland we had to drive through miles of parched Forest Service lands. There were firm restrictions on grazing federal lands, and the thick stands of uneaten grasses among the trees had long since turned brown. Any excuse of a spark could touch off an inferno. Already there were sixty thousand acres of wildfires charring Oregon and California.

My husband, Bruce, and our two twenty-something children were in the front seat. Nobody spoke much. We were all exhausted after spending the last ten hours building fence and doctoring cattle on our summer pasture. Numbly, in the half-sized backseat of the Ford pickup between two sleeping cow dogs and the remainder of our picnic lunch, I went over my list of things to do when we got home. If everything went right we could have supper by 9:45 PM.

Even when things were running smoothly we always had more to do than there were hours in a day. I prayed for help, but God never seemed to listen. Whatever I prayed for, I'd get the opposite. If I asked for a hammer, I'd get a teapot. I kept praying mostly because my mom believed in prayer. She'd died three years earlier, and praying made me feel a little closer to her.

I prayed for the rest of the afternoon to go smoothly: *Please make sure the Crock-Pot stayed on; I'm too tired to make dinner. Don't let the cows get out on the road. Don't let my daughter find any sick calves. Don't let my son flood out the hayfield. And make my husband get his irrigating done fast for once.* I finished with the usual: *Please keep my family safe. Amen.*

Wham!

What was that? Bruce jerked the wheel to straighten the pickup and brought it to a stop. "I think the left front tire blew out," he said. We'd only made it four miles from the summer pasture.

There was a collective groan as Bruce and the kids climbed out of the truck to fix the flat. I stayed in my seat between the dogs and glowered. *I pray to get home soon and You blow our tire. Whose side are You on, anyway? Don't You care about us?*

A movement in the field caught my attention. A ghostly gray tendril curled up from the ground, so faint I almost missed it.

"That's smoke!" I shouted, jumping out of my seat, startling the dogs. I joined Bruce and the kids at the side of the road and peered over the five-foot incline.

The tracks in the dust told the story plain as day. Someone had camped below the road. Beer cans and cigarette butts were strewn about. Worst of all, whoever it was had left their campfire still smoldering. Flames had crawled out of their crude fire pit and licked at the dry grasses. They were already spreading.

All we had was a gallon of water and two shovels.

My daughter, Susan, stomped the edges of the burning grass with her boots. Bruce smothered a large flare-up with his shovel. My son, Brandan, doused the embers of the campfire with the water. I called 911 on my cell phone. I couldn't believe I had a signal out here. Within minutes, three Forest Service crews arrived, lugging all the firefighting gear that was needed.

"Good thing you saw that, Mom," Susan said.

"A few more minutes and no one could have stopped it," Brandan agreed. The prevailing winds blew straight toward thousands of acres of vulnerable forests—not to mention our property.

Bruce grinned at me. "Good thing we blew the tire here, huh?"

"No," I said, smiling back. "God thing."

A RABBIT IN THE SNOW

by Julie Rae Pennertz

It was one of those dreadful nights we get here in Minnesota in the middle of winter. The moisture in the air gets trapped and a curtain of fog descends all around, mixing with the snow on the ground and the flurries falling from the sky to white out everything. Normally I wouldn't drive in that kind of weather, but I'd been at a Tupperware party all evening, I was eight months pregnant and I was so exhausted I just wanted to get home already.

I was only on the road for a minute before I regretted my decision not to stay put. The winding country road was totally deserted. My car's headlights couldn't penetrate the heavy fog and the snow was getting heavier. A lot heavier. Everything beyond a few feet in front of me was a mystery. I drove slowly. I wasn't quite sure where I was, though I knew the highway should be coming up pretty soon. Shivering, I cranked up the heat. The loud blowers did their work, cocooning me from the bitter cold outside. I prayed insistently for guidance.

All at once, a small animal darted out in front of me, just within the farthest arc of my headlights. I hit the brakes and came to a skidding stop.

It was a rabbit. A snowshoe rabbit, with frosty white fur and amber eyes. I inched the car forward, but the rabbit would not get out of the way. Instead, he darted back and forth about three feet in front of my car. I tapped the horn. Instead of hopping away like a rabbit would, he sat still and stared at me, his whiskered nose twitching. He was not going to let me pass. Come on, you silly rabbit, move, I thought a little impatiently.

At that moment the fog ahead swirled and lifted. A bright white light seemed to come from out of nowhere. The ground shook. A massive freight train roared by just a short distance beyond the stubborn sitting rabbit. Then, with one last twitch of his nose, the rabbit darted off out of sight.

On these country roads, rail crossings have no gates, no flashing lights. No way for a tired driver on a foggy winter's night to be warned of a speeding oncoming train. Except for a rabbit that behaved the way no normal rabbit ever would.

THE MIRACLE AT ARLONCOURT
by Amy Hogg Deull

What on earth was Dad looking for? He pressed his face against the car window, staring out at the Belgian countryside. Dad was on a mission to return to this place, yet he seemed anxious, as if there was something out there he dreaded seeing. But what? The only thing I'd been able to get out of him was that he wanted to drive to this tiny farm village, Arloncourt. Way off our planned itinerary. Now that we'd found it, I could see three streets, a small schoolhouse, and six other stucco buildings. Why were we here?

"Are you sure this is the right place?" I said.

Dad looked straight ahead, distracted. "This is it," he said, his voice barely above a whisper. "There's a road, a narrow lane that leads to a barn."

A barn? That's what we'd driven all this way to see?

We'd come to Belgium for the fiftieth anniversary of the Battle of the Bulge, where in the winter of 1944–45 the Allied forces, outnumbered and outgunned, withstood the Germans' last-gasp offensive surge. My dad, Charles Hogg, had been a tank gunner under Gen. George S. Patton in the famed 6th Armored Division. The Super Sixth, they were called. Growing up I listened wide-eyed to his stories of how they'd liberated starving families huddled in the cellars of their homes. How the fierce fighting had gone on for more than a month in the dead of winter, in the bitter cold, the snow and ice. The Germans hit them with everything they had, thousands of soldiers, hundreds of tanks, their most elite troops. All these little villages had been overrun, the Allied forces digging in, then slowly pushing the Nazis back against a barrage of artillery fire, rockets, bombs. Dad talked about how frightening it was. He was just a kid, barely twenty years old. In my eyes he seemed fearless. Tough as nails. The conquering hero.

But when the letter arrived inviting him to the official anniversary festivities in Belgium, Dad was adamant. He wasn't going. He came up with every excuse imaginable.

"I hate traveling. It's too far. I don't speak French. Besides, it's just too darn cold. I had enough of that." I looked at him, puzzled. I sensed there was something else that was bothering him, something he'd kept to himself all these years.

Finally he said, "Listen, I'm proud of what we did there, but there are things I'd just as soon not relive, things I've never told you about. That's all I'm going to say about it."

I let it drop. Then, just a few months before the anniversary, he called me. "I've been thinking about that trip to Belgium. Will you go with me?"

It wasn't like Dad to change his mind. At seventy, he was more stubborn, more set in his ways than ever. But I wasn't about to argue. I spent the weeks before we left boning up on my French.

We'd had a great time so far. Everywhere the veterans went the Belgian people rushed up, asking for autographs, thanking them. Children wanted to hold Dad's hand. Belgian radio and Dutch TV interviewed him. There had been solemn moments as well. Standing in the basement of a tavern where the SS had executed some thirty Belgian men and boys. Talking to children at an elementary school. The kids' simple, heartfelt questions had gotten Dad choked up, a lifetime of emotions stirring inside him.

But now? I didn't have a clue what Dad was up to. What was so important about a barn? What had he kept to himself all these years? *There are things I'd just as soon not relive.*

I got out of the car to look around. An older man walked toward me, a basket over his arm. "*Excusez moi,*" I said. "My father was here during the war. He's looking for a narrow lane that leads to a barn."

The man nodded, but didn't reply, sizing us up. He set his basket down and motioned for us to follow him. We came to a long, sloping farm road. In the distance, at the very end of the road, was a multistory barn.

"This is the place!" Dad said. Words tumbled out of his mouth. "Our tanks came down this road and across these fields, my tank in the lead. The Germans had just come through and we'd been given the order to clear the whole area. I was at the gun, watching."

I tried my best to translate for the farmer. *Char?* Was that the French word for *tank?*

"There was an outbuilding to the right," Dad continued. "We got out to search it. A wheelbarrow just outside the door. Inside it was a baby. Dead."

Dad's hands trembled as we walked toward the barn. With each sentence I wondered what might come next.

"We got back in the tank. I could see German tanks in the distance, there on the ridge. My gun was pointed right at the barn. We were maybe a hundred yards from it."

The farmer began talking at the same time as Dad, motioning, a flurry of gestures.

"The commander ordered me to rake the first floor of the barn with high-explosive shells," Dad went on. "He wanted it destroyed in case there were Germans hiding inside." Dad pantomimed opening the bolt of the gun, loading a shell.

"I hammered on the breech to push the shell into place. Like I'd done a thousand times before. It wouldn't budge. I pushed on it over and over. Slammed my fist against it. It was frozen solid. Why was this happening? Never once had I had a problem."

Tears fell from my father's eyes. "My commander was going crazy. 'Shoot! Shoot the gun, Hogg!' he screamed. 'Fire! Fire!' I pounded again with all my strength. Prayed that it would fire. And then—the door of the barn opened."

It was all Dad could do to get the words out. "People walked out with their arms in the air. 'Don't shoot,' they yelled. Not German soldiers. They were Belgians. Old men and women. Children. All of Arloncourt. Hiding, waiting until it was safe to come out. They never knew what had almost happened. I would have killed them all. I never said a word to them. We just drove on. The Germans were up on that ridge. I aimed, fired the gun. It went off without a problem. Like nothing had ever been wrong with it."

"I don't know what I thought would happen by coming here today. I was hoping—"

By then we were standing just feet from the barn. A young man sat atop a tractor. The older man related Dad's story. When he finished, the young man jumped off his tractor and ran into the barn. He returned with a middle-aged man, his father, as it turned out. "Thees ees heem," he said, pointing to Dad.

The father stood and stared at Dad. What was he going to do? Again Dad told the story, more with his hands than with words. This Belgian farmer understood perfectly. He'd been there in that very barn fifty years before, a small boy, terrified that he was going to die. Until Dad's gun inexplicably jammed.

Dad wrapped his arms around the man. They stood together in that winter field, the years falling away. I watched my father become transformed, as if a crushing weight had finally been lifted. All his life he must have been haunted by the question of "what if?" What if the gun hadn't failed? What if he had fired on those innocent people? Now he knew that a loving and protective power had intervened in the midst of a terrible battle. For years Dad had carried the spiritual wounds of that battle. Now, at last, he received healing.

"Thank you for our freedom," the son said in halting English. "Thank you that we are alive."

Dad nodded, wiped away his tears and embraced the young man.

Later I learned that the villagers had erected a small chapel. Called Our Lady of Deliverance, it commemorates the incredible events of that day, a day the people of Arloncourt will never forget. A day my father could finally remember with peace and gratitude. To him Arloncourt would always be sacred ground, a place where he'd experienced a miracle, not once, but twice.

IN A SILENT WAY
by Craig Pennington

I almost didn't see her. I was heading into Pittsburgh, across the bridge over the Allegheny River, late for work, and she was little more than a shadow by the seven-foot fence that lined the edge. But I got a feeling that I'd missed something. I tapped the brake, adjusted my rearview mirror. Then I saw what I had missed—a young woman climbing over.

I knew the stories about desperate souls who came to the bridge to take a fatal leap. Sometimes the police talked them out of it. Sometimes. I felt my throat clutch. I was the last person who should be on a bridge with a suicide jumper. I was beginning to think I couldn't do anything right. Just speaking up in class was hard enough. I was struggling to survive my sophomore year at the University of Pittsburgh. The only job I could get to support myself through school was at Burger King. And I was failing at that. This wasn't the first time I'd been late. My boss was fed up. "If you're late once more, you're fired," he had told me. "End of story."

I looked around. No other cars in sight. If I called the cops, would they get here in time? I had to do something. Now. But what? Why me? I pulled to the shoulder. *Lord, I'm such a screwup, I'm not who You want for this. But if You can give me the words to say, I'll say them. I'll try.*

My hands shook. I flipped on my emergency blinkers, zipped my jacket, and climbed out.

The jumper had scaled the fence, swung over, and was inching down the other side, dangling perilously over the dark, swirling water. Her long blonde hair blew in the bitter wind. She was young, probably only a few years older than me. Petite, dressed in a black hoodie, dark jeans, sneakers. Slowly, I approached. I didn't want to spook her. She was shivering violently, from the cold or fear or both. About ten feet away I glimpsed her face. Her makeup was smudged from tears. She turned. Her pale blue eyes locked with mine. Neither of us said anything. What could I say? One wrong word, and she could let go, plunging to her death.

Don't speak. Don't move. Listen. The words came to me as if from a third presence on the bridge. Time stopped. I was close enough to reach out and touch her hands, the knuckles white from clinging to the fence. But I didn't.

I've had enough. Her lips didn't move. But I heard her, through the lost look in her eyes. Her pain seemed to flow into me, and all at once I understood. Her troubles were deep, much deeper than mine, and yet they were the same. They came from fear and pain and hopelessness. But she didn't want to do this. *You just don't know what else to do,* I thought, and I knew she heard my thought. Somehow I was positive of that.

Suddenly I spoke out loud. "Climb to the top," I said. My voice sounded far away, like an echo. For a long moment she did nothing. Then one hand slid up, and the other. *That's it. Good, now step up.* She found a toehold.

Her arms started to shake. Our eyes locked again. I sent her another thought. *You will not fall.* She calmed down; her breathing slowed. Carefully, she made her way to the top. She paused, straddling the fence. Tears rolled down her cheeks. She looked so tiny and helpless. *I'm alone. I have no one.* I heard her thoughts as if they'd been spoken out loud.

"Will you come with me?" I asked, my voice again sounding like that strange echo. She nodded faintly, and lifted her other leg over to my side. She slid down to the pavement. Safe.

I took off my jacket. My size XL dwarfed her when she pulled it over her shoulders. "Would you like to sit in my car, where it's warm?" I asked. She nodded. We climbed into the car. I started the engine and cranked up the heat. The only sounds were the wind outside and the heat blowing.

But I heard her. *Please give me some time.* I waited silently while her emotions settled.

Finally I spoke. "I don't know your story and you don't have to tell me," I said. "May I call the police so I can make sure you are taken care of?"

It was a while before EMS and a squad car arrived. They escorted the woman into the ambulance and said they would notify her family. "How did you know what to say?" one officer asked me.

Say? I'd barely said anything. Everything had happened in a silent way. The officer scratched his head. "Well, whatever you did, kid, you did everything right."

Everything right. That was a first. It made me feel good, even if I couldn't explain it. There was a power out there on the bridge with us.

I got to Burger King two hours late. My boss met me at the door. "What are you doing here?" he asked, frowning, hands on his hips.

"I'm sorry I'm late again. I guess you're going to fire me," I said.

"Late? What do you mean, late? Your shift's tomorrow. You're not scheduled to work tonight."

CHAPTER 8

Revealed in Visions

MY SISTER'S GIFT
by Judith Preston

The salesclerk removed the pair of chandelier earrings from the glass case and dropped them in my waiting hands. They felt real, but I still had trouble believing it. Thin, hand-forged hoops and dangling, delicate chains, all in shimmering gold. I was mesmerized. Time seemed to stop. The department-store clatter faded into the background. Enraptured, I held one up to my ear and looked in the mirror. "A terrific Christmas gift," the clerk said, cheerily. "For your mother, maybe?"

The spell was broken. The crowd clustered by the shoes and handbags grew loud again. Out of the corner of my eye, I saw my mother walking over from the perfume counter. "They're... they're not for anybody," I murmured to the clerk. How could I explain to her when I couldn't even explain it myself? I hadn't told anybody about the dream, not even my mother.

It was the strangest dream I'd ever had, on the strangest, most terrible night. One month ago, close to midnight, I'd just returned home from a party when the phone rang. My mom was on the other end of the line, breathless, panicky. I held the receiver close to my ear, straining to make out her words.

"It's your sister," she said. "She had a brain aneurysm."

"I'm on my way," I said, reaching for my keys. It was snowing and the hospital was more than two hours away, but I had to see her. "There's no point risking the drive at this hour," my mother said. "The doctor says she's not going to wake up. Come in the morning."

I sat on the edge of my bed long after we hung up, desperate for sleep but scared of waking to a world without Jan. She was only forty-three. Never again would I hear her voice. Or sit at her kitchen table, eating home-baked treats from her little cookie tin. I crawled under my comforter. I wanted to talk to my sister again, but I wouldn't get the chance. Instead I spoke into the darkness: "Forgive me, Jan, if I've ever hurt you. I love you dearly."

Sleep came in fits and starts, one odd image breaking into my consciousness. A human ear—shaking, vibrating almost violently. The ear was pierced, and dangling from it was a beautiful gold earring, smooth, perfectly round hoops and fine, tightly linked chains. Was this Jan's way of letting me know she had heard me? The thought was as confusing as it was comforting.

Jan died five days later, never waking up. In those hard days that followed, it was the vision—strange as it was—that I held on to. I played the dream over and over in my head. The shaking ear and the dangly gold earring that adorned it.

Exactly like the pair of earrings the salesclerk had put in my hand. What did it mean?

"Find anything?" my mother said, joining me by the jewelry counter.

"These earrings," I said. I lifted them up so she could get a better look. "I...I had a dream about them. The night that Jan..."

Mom gasped and covered her face with her hands. She was so upset, I put my arm around her. "I'm sorry...," I began to say.

"Judith, you don't understand," my mother said. "I have those earrings at home. Jan bought them to give you for Christmas."

SHELTER FROM THE STORM
by Nikki McCurtain

A teacher's supposed to have the answers. I can teach my fourth graders the state capitals and how to write cursive; I can list all the books in C. S. Lewis's *Chronicles of Narnia* series. But I can't explain why some children died in the tornado that hit our school last May and the ones with me survived. All I can tell you is that the tragedy doesn't mean God was absent.

My colleagues and I went back three weeks later to see the devastation where Plaza Towers Elementary once stood. Most of the debris had been hauled away. We brought chalk and Sharpies to write on the remaining rubble, a way to say good-bye. I stepped over concrete blocks to where my classroom had been.

"The best class ever," I scrawled on the dusty linoleum. My first class, my first full year of teaching. I never imagined it ending like this. From here I could see the path we'd taken, down the hall and into the bathroom, our shelter from the storm. I remembered everything.

The Sunday before the storm, I was in our living room, getting things together for school. Tornado warnings had run on TV all weekend. They're a fact of life here in Oklahoma, and our school frequently ran tornado drills. But I had never been in a twister's path. The thought terrified me. I was trained to teach and respond to a disaster, but was I ready? Every weather update increased my anxiety. Lives were in my hands. What if I faltered under pressure when my students needed me most?

I was putting away some manila folders when it happened. I looked up, and the living room wall seemed to melt away. In its place was an image of destruction. I could see myself walking in debris: wood, dirt, glass, bricks. I closed my eyes, wishing the vision away. I opened them. It was still there. The disaster had come. And I wasn't brave, I was completely paralyzed.

I called to my husband. "Preston, come here!" He came running. I rubbed my eyes; the image vanished. "Something bad is going to happen," I told him, hardly able to breathe. And I was powerless to stop it.

"We should pray about it," Preston said.

All at once, Psalm 91 came to mind. In my Bible study, we'd been analyzing it. "He will cover you with His pinions, and under His wings you will find refuge...."

Pinions, we'd learned, were the strongest feathers in a bird's wing, able to withstand the most pressure without breaking. The psalm wasn't just about protection—it was about making us strong in the face of danger. That's what I needed. Preston and I prayed, and I felt my courage rising.

Monday at school started out quiet, but the tornado warnings persisted. In the afternoon, I gathered my children around me to read Lewis's *The Magician's Nephew*, but didn't get far.

"All teachers and students, please seek safety immediately," our principal announced over the intercom. "Tornado drill." The sky was dark, lightning flashed, thunder roared, hail pelted the roof. In the distance, sirens wailed.

This is no drill. I felt the panic, the paralysis creep in. But I remembered I had to draw on God's strength. "Follow me, students," I said to my class. I led them into the hall, just as we'd drilled. The other teachers and I debated whether to take an additional step—cramming into the bathrooms, which at least were away from the windows. I spoke up, as did some others. "Let's go." Forty of us crowded in. Some crawled under sinks, some huddled in stalls.

The approaching tornado was deafening. The ground shook. The power flickered, and the light streaming in from the hallway faded. The air smelled dank, rotten.

My phone rang. Preston! I held it to my ear. "Nikki," he said, "I love you." "I love you too," I shouted back. The line went dead. Then the power went out completely.

My fear was so great I couldn't think of what to do. Then those words from Psalm 91 came to me, the lines I'd prayed with Preston. "Crouch down," I urged the children. "Backpacks and books over your heads. Fold your legs under you. Keep your backs to the wall." I sank down by the doorway. One girl started crying. I threw my arms around her.

I prayed, calling out to the screaming winds, "He will cover you with His pinions, and under His wings you shall find refuge.…" Others prayed too.

The air pressure plummeted. Walls crashed, the roof lifted up, pipes broke, shards of metal and concrete flew. The wind sucked the air out of my lungs. I kept praying. Then I felt a hand against my back. Someone comforting me. I glanced up. No one was there. I shut my eyes again.

The hail stopped, the whipping winds ceased. The next time I looked up, there was nothing but sky above us. I peered out the doorway. The hall wasn't there anymore.

We stepped carefully over the concrete blocks and bricks. First responders guided us out, holding our hands. I looked over the debris. Fallen beams, rain-soaked insulation, shattered glass. Devastation no one could have been prepared for.

Yet I'd seen it before, that Sunday. Everything, the awesome destruction, laid out before me. I had been ready. When the tornado came, I'd done what I thought I couldn't—what I needed to do.

I wanted to thank God for that. So I'd come back, weeks after the disaster, Sharpie in hand. I walked through the rubble to the bathroom. I knew what I wanted to write, what I had to say. The only answer I had found amid all the unanswerable questions. But the words were already written there by someone else. "Under His wings you shall find refuge.…"

I don't know why terrible things happen. But I know how we get through them. We are covered by pinions, the strongest feathers, ready to face whatever comes next.

GOD WILL TAKE CARE OF YOU
by Idella Edwards

The day after my mother's funeral I sat on her bed, thankful that my three daughters were helping me sort through her things. I could hardly touch a piece of her clothing without breaking down in tears. I had tried to make her service a glorious, beautiful tribute to her hundred years of life and unshakable faith—but had I honored her the way she would have wanted? I second-guessed everything. Especially the final hymn I chose: "God Will Take Care of You." I wasn't even sure why I'd picked it.

Music was a huge part of Mother's life, interwoven with her faith. Nothing brought her more joy than entertaining folks with a sing-along, playing boogie-woogie or a hymn on the piano. So when it came time to choose the songs for her service my mind flashed back to the hundreds of selections she'd performed over the years. I hoped I'd made the right choice.

"Wow!" one of my daughters said, jolting me from my thoughts. "Look at all those papers."

I got up off the bed and knelt on the floor in front of a plastic tub that held a bundle of documents. My curiosity took over. What were these papers? Were they notes from my late father? Her childhood friends? I pulled one sheaf out at random and read.

"Years ago I was planning a road trip, so I traded in my old car for another, better, used one. That same night I had a dream." *A dream?* I read on. "I was driving along the highway when suddenly I had to turn my car sharply to the right. *Bam!* The right front tire blew out and I went up and over an embankment.

"The next morning I awoke with a start, terribly worried about the tires on my new car. I drove it to an auto-body shop. 'I'm planning a road trip next week. Do you think my tires are in good shape for it?' I asked the mechanic.

"He checked out all the tires and came back to the lobby. 'Ma'am, all of your tires are worn—especially that front right one. We've got to change them straight away.'

"'You're kidding,' I said. A shiver ran down my spine. I bought four brand-new tires.

"The following week I set out on my road trip. I was driving along when all at once an oncoming car veered into my lane! I turned sharply to the right just like I had in my dream...only this time my tire didn't blow out. I was totally fine. Totally protected."

I was amazed. Mom had never told any of us this story. She'd probably written it down, planning to submit it somewhere, but never got around to it. I finished reading.

"And that's why to this day my very favorite hymn is 'God Will Take Care of You,' because I know, without a doubt, that God protects me. He protects us all."

And now I knew that my choice of hymn had been the right one.

I DREAMED OF A DROWNING
by April Depuy

I walk leisurely up the steep, narrow, rugged path high above a roaring river. I've been here before. I feel sure of it. The stately evergreen trees and the water are familiar. J, my sixty-pound border collie, lopes along beside me, my trusted companion.

I stop to take a picture of the river, looking down over a sheer rock face. The water is a brilliant turquoise blue, except for the white of the rapids, crashing violently over jagged rocks.

J goes on ahead of me. I'm not worried. She's well trained. Smart and obedient.

I hear a scampering noise. I turn and see J jump, her body falling, falling to the river below.

I freeze, paralyzed with fear. Finally, I look down. But J is nowhere to be found. I scan every inch of the river. It's no use. She's gone. Why did I hesitate? Why? I feel helpless and guilty.

For an instant I wasn't sure where I was. Everything around me was suddenly dark. I reached under me and felt...my bed. Thank God. Just a dream. But the same dream. Again.

I felt sweat running down my neck. I looked for J. She was stretched out on the floor, sleeping, with Bo, my other border collie, beside her. Their chests rose and fell. Everything was fine.

But why did I keep having this nightmare? It was so real, so frighteningly vivid. I couldn't get that horrible moment out of my mind—being frozen, watching my dog disappear in the rapids.

My husband, Don, lay peacefully beside me. I reached over and shook him awake.

"*Wh-h-hat?*" he said. "What's wrong?"

"I had that dream again," I said. "I'm scared. What would I do if that really happened? If something bad happened to J I'd never forgive myself."

He wrapped an arm around me and held me against him. "Nothing's going to happen," he said. "It was just a weird dream."

I sighed. If only I knew what to do. But I didn't. That was the problem. I didn't have a clue. I felt the warmth of Don's hand on my shoulder and drifted back to sleep.

I was a little better the next morning. The sun streaked through the blinds as the dogs shot out the back door. But I was afraid to let them out of my sight. A week went by. Then another. No dream. Spring gave way to summer; the memory of those strange, haunting visions faded. I finally relaxed.

That July I invited Jamie, a girlfriend, to spend a long weekend with me and the dogs at a cabin by the Metolius River in central Oregon. We hiked the mountain trails and took photos of wildflowers. In the evening we cooked out, while the dogs swam in the nearby river, the water swift, but not treacherous. It felt great to kick back.

The last day we decided to go check out a fish hatchery upstream from our cabin. We leashed the dogs and walked over a bridge near the hatchery. I stopped to admire the gentle rapids below, the water the most incredible shade of turquoise. I spied a trail that ran beside the river. "Let's go," I said.

At the trailhead J and Bo strained at their leashes. They wanted to play. "Okay, you two, don't get into trouble." I unclipped them. I felt a flicker of unease as the dogs loped in front of us up the trail.

We reached a spot where the rapids crashed over huge rocks. The now raging current was breathtaking. We stopped to take a photo. I lowered my camera and looked at Jamie. Bo was right beside her. But where was J? I called for her, but there was no answer.

Frantic, I scanned the river. Suddenly J's head popped up, like a seal's, about seven feet upstream. She'd jumped in, probably thinking the water here was as mellow as it was near the cabin. But it wasn't. The current pulled her under.

I didn't hesitate. I jumped into the water. So cold it took my breath away. Just then I felt something rush past my hand. J. I grabbed her collar, but it was all I could do to hold on. I pulled her head up out of the water and held her tight. The force of the rapids threatened to suck us both downstream. We bounced against some rocks and I found my footing.

I eased my leg from between two of the rocks and stumbled out of the water, still holding on to J. She didn't have a scratch on her. I leashed the dogs and we slowly made our way back to my pickup. I had a sore knee, but it didn't really bother me. In a way it was almost reassuring. My badge of courage. How had I possibly managed to get ahold of J's collar? Another second and she would have been gone, swept through those vicious rapids.

"I can't believe you jumped in like that!" Jamie said. "It all happened so fast. But you weren't even scared. It was like you knew exactly what you had to do. Like you'd seen it before."

I had, hadn't I?

A PICTURE OF HEAVEN
by Cathy Ahl

Warm, glowing lights. Music, joyful and familiar. What was the tune? Where was it coming from? Where was I? I felt so safe, so loved. Strong arms enveloped me. I looked up. *Dad!* We were dancing together the way we did when I was a little girl. The way we did at my wedding. But Dad was gone now. How could we be dancing? How could he be here at all?

I searched his face for an answer. He smiled and suddenly none of it seemed strange at all. It was as real as anything I'd ever experienced. "I love you," he said with his eyes, his very presence. For the first time in months my heart wasn't weighted down by grief. Dad wasn't gone. He was happy and he wanted me to be happy too.

I opened my eyes to the morning sun in my bedroom. The dream faded away, but the feeling stayed with me. *Dad was here,* I thought. *It was really him.* He'd come to me to let me know he was all right.

I jumped out of bed—I had to tell Mom. She knew how much I missed Dad, how upset I'd been for so long, angry at God for taking a good man so young—only fifty-two years old—after a short battle with cancer. In my grief I couldn't believe there was any meaning to it. I knew Mom grieved too. She'd lost the love of her life. And yet her faith sustained and comforted her.

"Do you really believe in heaven, Mom?" I'd asked her one day as we sat in her kitchen. "Do you really think there's anything after we die?"

Mom patted my hand. "Honey, all I think about lately are the wonderful times your dad and I spent on the beach in Florida. Remember those days?"

Of course I did. Mom and Dad went to Clearwater Beach every year. They spent hours walking the shore collecting seashells, Mom in her sunglasses and Dad in his favorite floppy, crumpled blue hat—picture-perfect beachcombers.

"I think about the white sand, the sun, the hugs and kisses we shared, and all those seashells we collected, and I'm sure there is a heaven. Your dad and I saw a glimpse of it here on earth," Mom said. "God would not have given us those moments if there wasn't something greater awaiting us."

"But how can you just believe that?" I said. "We can't know what happens after we die. All I know is that Dad's not here anymore."

Mom put her hands on my shoulders. "Before your dad died he promised to try to send me a sign when he got to heaven to let me know he was okay. He never broke a promise to me. I believe that one day God will send me a sign that your father is safe with Him."

Could it be that my strange, wonderful dream was that sign? I rushed over to Mom's house to tell her.

"I had the strangest dream...," I began, but Mom interrupted.

"Sit down," she said. The urgency in her voice puzzled me, but I did what I was told. "I want to show you something," she continued. "I just got this in the mail." She handed me a travel magazine that her credit card company had sent its customers. "Look," she said, opening to a feature section on Clearwater Beach, Florida—Mom's heaven on earth. I flipped through the glossy pages to an article called "Shelling." The pictures were gorgeous—seashells of all varieties, endless stretches of sand and sea and sky. "Turn the page," Mom said softly.

A wide shot spread across two pages. A lovely view of Clearwater Beach. In the foreground a man was bending over to pick up a seashell. A man in a funny, crumpled blue hat.

"Dad?" I gasped. It *was* Dad, plain as day. And beyond him, in orange pants, not quite in focus, was Mom. Caught by a travel photographer's camera without their knowing.

"Now I know," Mom said, running her fingers over the page. "Dad's in heaven for sure. He got there first, but one day I'll be there too." Mom closed the magazine and looked into my eyes. "Now that I've got my sign, do you believe?"

"I do, Mom," I told her. "You see, I received a sign as well...."

MAN OF MY DREAMS
by Kamilah Dozier

What kind of party was this?

I'd been to plenty of parties in my life—maybe *too* many—and they were nothing like this. My sister Chinue and her friends from church sat around her apartment, talking and laughing over soda and chips. There was no drinking, no drugs, no one hooking up. It was so...*wholesome*. I didn't have their faith. I didn't have any faith, actually. The idea of God always raised more questions than answers for me.

But I didn't hate this party. The people actually wanted to talk about their feelings! And there was no chance here that I'd find some guy who wasn't good for me. I'd dated enough Mr. Wrongs already.

"It was great meeting you," one of Chinue's friends said as she left. "Maybe I'll see you at our church sometime."

Me? I thought. *At your church? No thanks!*

I went home and crawled into bed. And dreamed. I dreamed I was in a room decorated in black. Like a nightclub. *Where am I?* I wondered. I'd never seen this club before. There was no dancing. No guys and girls in club clothes. The people around me separated into little groups to talk. Suddenly the scene shifted. I was in a cabin. *Camping trip?* I thought, feeling the slats of a bunk bed and breathing in the scent of cedar and pine. Hanging in the sky outside the window was the biggest golden moon I'd ever seen. I gazed up at it and someone whispered in my ear, "This is the man you are going to marry."

Man? What man? There was no man. *Weird.* That's when I woke up.

And just as quickly the strangest urge came over me: *Go to Chinue's and make breakfast.* It was more than a thought—it was a command. *Must have been because of that party,* I thought, getting out of bed. I hadn't been planning to go over to Chinue's today. Now it seemed like something I just had to do.

Chinue was surprised to see me and invited me in. Soon I found myself telling her about my weird dream. "Whoever heard of a club like that?" I said.

Chinue blinked at me over her eggs. "Have you ever been to our midweek?" she asked.

"Your what?"

"My church holds midweek services in a place called the Upside Down Club. It looks exactly like the place you described. We have a service and then we always break up into groups to talk." *Really crazy.*

"Next you'll be telling me you do camping trips. That was in my dream too."

"As a matter of fact, we're having a singles camping trip in two weeks," Chinue said.

What kind of coincidence was this?

Two weeks later I was lying in the very same top bunk as in my dream. I even checked out the window for my giant golden moon, but the sky was black. The people at the camp weren't like any people I'd ever met. All that talk about God! I didn't understand a lot of it and felt out of place, but I stuck it out. I prayed, I sang, even got up the nerve to speak at a service. "I'm really glad to be here," I confessed to over a hundred other campers. "But I'm terrified of all of you!"

Afterward, this guy Tori, a friend of Chinue's, came up to me. "I really related to what you said about fear. I've had a lot of that in my life," he told me. What kind of guy was this?

Tori and I stayed in touch. Nothing romantic. Just two friends who each wanted happiness for the other. Then, after a year, Tori asked me to be his girlfriend. On our first official date we went to the Santa Monica pier. It all seemed perfect—and that made me nervous. Really nervous. Was I going to lose a friend trying to make him into something else? Then I looked up. There it was, hanging in the newly darkened sky: the giant golden moon from my dream, bigger than any moon I'd ever seen, bigger than the sun itself, seemingly.

What kind of miracle was this?

Tori and I have been married for ten years now. As for my doubts about God, you could say I found the answers to all my questions.

BUT WHAT ABOUT ME?

by Jack Brewer

All these years I've never forgotten it. People might say that it was just a dream, but I can tell you that boy who appeared in the early morning darkness at the foot of my bed was as real as anything I'd ever seen. I could have reached out and touched him. Shaken his hand, asked him about his schoolwork. But in an instant he was gone and all that was left were shadows and moonlight and the certainty that someone was trying to tell me something. If I'd only listen.

I'd gone out to the boondocks of Hockley, Texas, on the insistence of Mr. Robinson, a businessman who was the head of a facility for troubled boys. He wanted me to become its first executive director. He had leaned across the restaurant table where we were having lunch and said, "You will never serve in a place that needs you more."

The program was failing, and if it did, those boys would have nowhere to go. They'd be back on the streets. I told him I was totally unqualified. I'd never done anything like it. I'd been a youth pastor for ten years, working with well-reared kids from good homes. "I don't know a thing about helping troubled youth," I said.

Ever since I had been called to the ministry I'd been pretty clear about what my gifts were. Besides, I had a wife and three kids to support. Why would I uproot them from our home by the Gulf to go to this lonely ranch in the middle of nowhere?

Just to appease Mr. Robinson—and my conscience—I took a day off and drove to the place, north of Houston. Everything I saw convinced me I was right. This was too much for me. A half-finished, half-abandoned dorm of concrete blocks. A chicken house with a rabbit hutch inside and a hog pen filled with grunting, snorting, mud-encrusted hogs. Actually, the hogs looked like the best-fed residents there.

My guide clearly wished to get off the ranch as soon as he could.

"Let me show you where the boys sleep," he said. We walked into a double-wide and I caught my breath at the smell. There were rows of World War II–vintage steel bunks. I opened the door of one of the plywood cabinets. Cockroaches swarmed over the shelves. "The bathroom's in the back." I found some dripping showers and a stopped-up commode. No wonder it stank.

"You should see where they eat," he said. I followed him to another trailer and glanced in: oilcloth-covered folding tables hosting a few flies and a spattered coffeepot. A dozen boys lounged outside, smoking cigarettes. Two of them dangled from a rope swing. "Howdy," I said. All I got were grunts and shrugs. They knew the program's days were numbered.

"It would take a miracle to save this place," my guide said.

I drove back home. Called Mr. Robinson to be polite. "Will you take the job?" he asked.

"I'll pray about it," I said. Then Carolyn and the kids piled into our car and we went to our country place. It was bluebonnet season and our cabin was floating in an ocean of them. The kids romped around, playing tag and catch. "Don't worry," I told Carolyn. "No way am I going to take that job."

We slept that night with the windows open, the warm breeze heavy with the sweet scent of bluebonnets. I woke early, my wife sleeping silently beside me. *Lord*, I prayed, *don't ever lead me to a place like that.* So much for my promise to pray about it. God knew what I could do, and fixing that mess was not on the list.

Then the boy appeared. He gazed at me from beneath a mop of black hair, his dark eyes searching. He was dressed in a mismatched pair of plaid pants and a plaid shirt.

"But what about me?" he asked.

What about me? Was he one of the boys I'd seen on the rope swing or smoking cigarettes outside that ratty trailer? Was he one of the ones who had barely returned my "Howdy"? Where had he come from? He looked younger than those boys, lonely, yearning for help. I blinked, shook my head. Looked again. He was still there. Not just a figment of my imagination or a dream but real, staring right at me. I bolted upright, ready to demand what he was doing there.

Carolyn tossed in bed. "Honey, are you okay?"

I turned toward her. "Go back to sleep," I whispered. I didn't want to frighten her.

I looked back. The boy was gone.

For the next twenty-four hours I did some of the hardest thinking I'd ever done. Where did God want me? Why did that boy come to me? How would I do a job that I was totally unprepared for? That I would fail at? Even before I talked to Carolyn it all seemed pretty clear. That question. *What about me?* It was an answer to a prayer I hadn't said, that I was afraid to say. But now I knew. I had to go. I had to help those boys.

I called Mr. Robinson, quit my church job. We sold our house and moved out to the boondocks. Running Boys Country, a Christian home for boys, was one of the hardest things I'd ever done. No, it was impossible. I faced one hopeless challenge after another, finding staff, raising money, building new facilities to make the boys feel safe and at home. And yet, whenever we asked for something, God somehow heard us.

We needed a cook. Along came Big Mama. We needed someone with a passion for working with kids. Charles Green appeared. Even small details fell into place. One evening I told God that we wanted to provide a treat to the boys after dinner, but couldn't figure out what. To my amazement, I'd barely finished saying grace when a truck driver pulled up from something called Mrs. Shelby's Cookie Company. "We thought you might like some cookies," he said.

Six months to the day after I took that job, an elderly couple visited the ranch with their grandson. They'd seen an ad I'd run in the Baptist paper. The only ad I ever ran in all my years at Boys Country. "We need to find a place for David," they said. The grandfather took me aside and explained that they feared they weren't long for this earth. They wanted to know their grandson would be well cared for.

They introduced him to me. A shy, smart, dark-haired ten-year-old boy. He looked up at me, those dark eyes and mop of black hair unmistakably familiar. It was the boy I'd seen that night. The very same boy.

David was an excellent student. Loved animals and knew everything about butterflies and birds. Had his own pet pigeon. But he was just one of so many boys—and, later, girls—who thrived at what became Boys and Girls Country. For twenty-two years I served as executive director and watched the place grow from a few acres to 160, with dozens of classrooms, cottages, dorms, a chapel. We received award after award and I found a new calling.

All because of a boy's question that came in response to a feeble prayer one bluebonnet-scented night: *What about me?*

ONE LAST MESSAGE
by Steve Erlanger

The house was quiet. Clinking silverware was about the only sound my wife, Elaine, and I made at dinner anymore, and sitting outside on the patio afterward, it seemed like even the crickets spoke in hushed tones. I longed to hear rock music booming from upstairs, or the rattle of skateboard wheels on our driveway. Elaine glanced up at the dark balcony overlooking the patio and I followed her gaze. *Stop it,* I thought. It had been six months since the motorcycle accident that killed our sixteen-year-old son, Austin, and it was time to stop looking for ghosts. The silence was haunting enough, a pervasive reminder of his absence.

Elaine began to cry. I moved close to comfort her. But what could I say? She couldn't let him go. Any more than I could. Neither of us could fill that aching void that Austin's death left. What parent could? Often, Elaine told me she had visions of him. The night after he died, she said he came to her in a dream so real that she felt his touch. "He's reaching out to us," she said. "I know it. He wants to comfort us. That's the way Austin was."

I wasn't so sure. As a newspaper publisher for sixteen years, my job was to collect facts, evidence. Report on things objectively. All I could see was that empty balcony where Austin would stand before going to bed and shout, "I love you guys!"

The memory brought tears to my eyes. The last thing Elaine needed was to see me lose it. "I'll get you some tissues," I said, and went inside to our bedroom. I spoke into the darkness. "Son, we're suffering. If you're reaching out, let us know you're okay."

I composed myself and returned to the patio. Elaine had stopped crying. "Your phone buzzed," she said. On the patio table, my phone flashed.

A text. I didn't recognize the number. I clicked on it and saw there was a document attached.

"Do you know this number?" I asked, showing Elaine the phone.

"It's so familiar," she said, studying it. Then she froze. "It's Austin."

Impossible. We'd cancelled his account.

I couldn't open the attachment on my phone. All I could see was the header: IMGOO.

"I'm good...," Elaine suggested, her voice a whisper.

I forwarded the message to my computer in the den. Now we saw that IMG was the file name for an image: 001, 002 and so on. Elaine leaned in close. I could feel her heart pounding as I clicked on the first attachment.

A photo popped on screen: a picture of my father—Austin's grandfather—to whom Austin had been extraordinarily close. It had been a year to the day—exactly—since Dad had died. Another photo loaded up, and another—twenty in total. Austin jumping on a skateboard. Austin on the patio, playacting the balcony scene from *Romeo and Juliet* with his girlfriend. Austin photographing himself in a mirror. As Elaine and I flipped through them, the house seemed to fill with his presence.

There had to be some logical explanation. Had someone gotten hold of Austin's cell phone? I checked the kitchen cabinet. There it was, switched off, sealed in a plastic bag, untouched, exactly as we had left it six months earlier. That night I could barely sleep. *Lord,* I prayed, *are You trying to reassure us?*

First thing the next morning I drove to the AT&T store. "Has this number been reassigned?" I asked a salesman.

He looked it up on his computer. "No, sir, it's out of service. No one has it."

Not long after, Elaine came to me with another dream about Austin. This time, he'd come with a message. "He said, 'Tell Dad I know. Tell Dad I heard him,'" Elaine said. "Does that make any sense to you?"

No logical sense, no. Elaine couldn't know about the plea I had made in our bedroom, alone. But I'm a believer in what I witness. And what I know now is that our son isn't gone. Not forever. He's someplace else, and he's "good."

THE LIGHTNING SONATA
by Tony Cicoria

The concert hall is dark and still, all eyes on the lone figure at the center of the stage. The piano player. I creep up behind him, careful not to disturb the soft plink-plink *of the keys. This melody he's playing—it's beautiful. Unlike anything I've ever heard before. The closer I get, the more familiar the man becomes. I recognize him. The piano player is me. The music? It's mine.*

The same melody echoed in my head nearly fifteen years later as I took my seat at the grand piano in front of hundreds at the Goodrich Theater in Oneonta, New York, my hometown. I could remember the notes as if I'd dreamed them up yesterday. I *had* dreamed them up, in the dream that haunted me to this day. As did the literal bolt from the blue that started it all.

It was just an ordinary summer day. Not a cloud in the sky. I'd driven up to a lake in Athens, New York, that morning for my wife's family reunion. The kids were splashing in the lake and I was grilling up burgers and hot dogs. What could be better? My medical practice was booming, the family was happy. Life was good.

I slipped away to make a call to my mom on a pay phone by a lakeside pavilion, oblivious of the storm clouds on the horizon. The phone rang six, eight times. The wind kicked up. A woman and her daughter waited behind me. I was about to hang up when *boom!* A bolt of lightning struck the pavilion, coursed through the receiver and shocked me square in the face with terrifying force, sending me flying fifteen feet.

What happened next is a blur. It sounds nuts, but I was submerged in this hazy blue-white light. Like I'd fallen into a peaceful river. I could sense something overwhelming, powerful but loving. God? I wasn't sure, but I never wanted to leave. Fifteen minutes later, though, I awoke to a woman pumping my chest, jolting me back to life. The same woman who'd been standing behind me at the pay phone. She was an ICU nurse.

Three weeks later, I was back at work. My doctors had conducted all the routine neurological exams and concluded I was fine. Only something was off—way off. I had this strange compulsion to listen to classical piano music. The kind that had put me to sleep as a kid the year my mom forced me to take piano lessons.

"I can't explain it," I confided to a doctor friend. "It's like I *crave* it."

This from a guy who'd spent the previous two decades roaring around on a Harley and blasting out the Rolling Stones. I bought a Chopin CD just to test the waters, feeling like an imposter in the classical section of the music store. But as soon as I played it, I was hooked. I hummed to Chopin in the car, at work, even at the dinner table. When I wasn't listening to the music, I was thinking about it. Obsessively. I was a practical guy, a doctor, not some New Age hippie who spent his time chasing *ooey-ooey* feelings from the great unknown. Was I going crazy? Is that what the bolt of lightning had done?

It only got weirder. A week later, our babysitter stopped by. She was moving and needed a favor. "Dr. Cicoria, I have this old piano," she said. "I can't take it with me. Can you keep it for a while? A year, tops?"

As soon as we moved the piano into our house, the dream came—me in a concert hall, performing a sonata I'd somehow composed. Me, who had virtually no musical training. It jolted me awake, the music still ringing in my head. I could hear whole chunks of it, like someone had downloaded a file directly into my brain. This was getting ridiculous. I buried my head in my pillow, but the notes begged and pleaded to come out.

Enough was enough. I tiptoed downstairs, sat at the creaky piano bench and tried to mimic the melody. The moment I plucked out a few soft notes it hit me. That same powerful sense of love and peace. The lightning bolt had coursed through my body with a force that should have killed me, but instead, it had left something beautiful behind. That beauty wasn't meant to stay inside my head. I knew nothing about composing, but I knew exactly what I had to do—follow that music.

That's how I'd ended up in a real concert hall, after years of piano lessons and practicing into the wee hours of the night to release the music within.

A hush fell over the crowd. I couldn't stop trembling—until my fingers finally found the keys and the music took over.

When I finished, I took a bow as the audience erupted into thunderous applause. All in response to the piece I'd composed—"The Lightning Sonata."

CRISIS AT 37,000 FEET
by Debi Lammert

I heard the cry. My heart dropped. *No!* I thought, *not now!* I eased the little
boy, named Mustafah, from his panicked mother. His body was limp. His
skin was gray. His tiny chest heaved. I'm a nurse, and I knew what that
meant: Mustafah was in a full-blown Tet spell—a life-threatening episode
of low blood oxygen. We were thirty-seven thousand feet over the Atlantic,
on a plane from Bosnia to New York. And today, Good Friday, we'd need
a miracle if he was going to survive up here.

I grabbed an oxygen tank from an overhead bin and fitted the mask
over his face.

I'd been worried about this trip from the get-go. I'm a volunteer medical escort for the Samaritan's Purse Children's Heart Project. We help
transport sick kids and their parents from their home countries to North
America for treatment. A few days before our flight I met the folks I'd be
helping—two babies and their mothers—and their translator.

Seventeen-month-old Mustafah was a problem. He had a complex
heart defect called Tetralogy of Fallot that can cause fatal Tet spells.

Holding Mustafah I clung to a single hope: My church back home in
Tulsa, Oklahoma, had our flight schedule. "We'll be totally covering you
in prayer," Nancy, our prayer group leader, told me before I left. "Try not
to worry."

So far I hadn't had anything to worry about. Our flight from Sarajevo to
Vienna was smooth. Then we settled in for the nine-hour transatlantic haul.
Mustafah played in the bulkhead area until he got tired. Four hours in, after
beverages and a meal, the plane fell quiet, the lights dimmed and the flight
attendants retired to the back of the plane. It was about 11:00 PM.

Then Mustafah cried out, in the grip of the Tet spell.

I got the oxygen flowing and gave him a drug to relax the blood vessels to his lungs. Then I did all that there was left to do—pray. The translator joined me. "Please, Lord," we pleaded, "don't let him die." I checked Mustafah's vitals every minute. No change. *Please, please, please...* Five minutes, ten, twenty. The most intense twenty minutes I'd ever experienced, like twenty lifetimes. One second I thought I'd lost him, the next, he was back. Then came a small increase in his oxygen level. His breathing stabilized. He fell into a deep, natural sleep. By the time we arrived in New York, he was smiling like nothing had happened. Crisis over. Just like that. I was almost as dumbfounded as I was relieved.

The next day Nancy called from church. "How'd it go?" she asked. "Everyone okay?"

"Yes," I said, "the kids are fine. Their treatments begin today."

"That's wonderful, Debi," she said. "I was so worried. I have to tell you about yesterday. I got to church for the five o'clock Good Friday service and felt this sudden, overwhelming urge to pray at the altar. Almost like a vision, I saw a toddler boy lying unconscious in your arms. Near death. Desperate. I kept repeating, over and over, *Lord, please don't let this child die. Please don't let him die!* I lost track of time. Before I knew it, twenty minutes had passed. So had the urge to pray. Just like that. I practically went limp."

When I hung up the phone, I did the math.

Five o'clock in Tulsa was eleven o'clock where we had been, over the Atlantic.

A NOTE FROM THE EDITORS

Explore More Stories
of God's Comfort & Grace

Enjoy these other books filled with true stories
that dispel doubt and fear, and show how
God never stops embracing you.

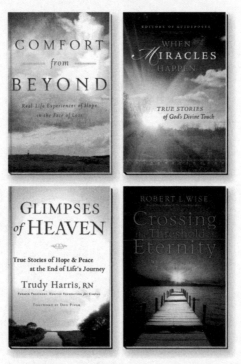

To learn more about these books,
visit ShopGuideposts.org

**Receive even more inspiration when you
sign up for weekly newsletters at
Guideposts.org/newsletters**